The Underground Railroad: Next Stop, Toronto!

Adrienne Shadd • Afua Cooper • Karolyn Smardz Frost

NATURAL HERITAGE BOOKS
TORONTO

The Underground Railroad: Next Stop, Toronto!
Adrienne Shadd, Afua Cooper & Karolyn Smardz Frost

Published by Natural Heritage / Natural History Inc.
P.O. Box 95, Station O, Toronto, Ontario M4A 2M8

www.naturalheritagebooks.com

National Library of Canada Cataloguing in Publication

Shadd, Adrienne L. (Adrienne Lynn)
   The underground railroad : next stop, Toronto! / Adrienne Shadd, Afua Cooper & Karolyn Smardz Frost.

Includes bibliographical references and index.
ISBN 1-896219-86-1

1. Black Canadians — Ontario — Toronto — History — 19th century. 2. Black Canadians — Ontario — Toronto — Social life and customs — 19th century.
3. Underground railroad — Canada. 4. Toronto (Ont.) — History — 19th century.
I. Cooper, Afua II. Smardz, Karolyn III. Title.

FC3097.9.B6C65 2002   971.3'541'00496   C2002-904991-1
F1059.5.T689N32 2002

Cover and text design by Sari Naworynski
Edited by Jane Gibson
Printed and bound in Canada by Hignell Printing Limited, Winnipeg, Manitoba

Front cover image: From William Still, *The Underground Rail Road* (1872) Opp. 125. Toronto Public Library, Special Collections, Genealogy & Maps Centre.

Natural Heritage / Natural History Inc. acknowledges the financial support of the Canada Council for the Arts and the Ontario Arts Council for our publishing program. We also acknowledge the financial support of the Government of Canada through the Book Publishing Industry Development Program (BPIDP) and the Association for the Export of Canadian Books.

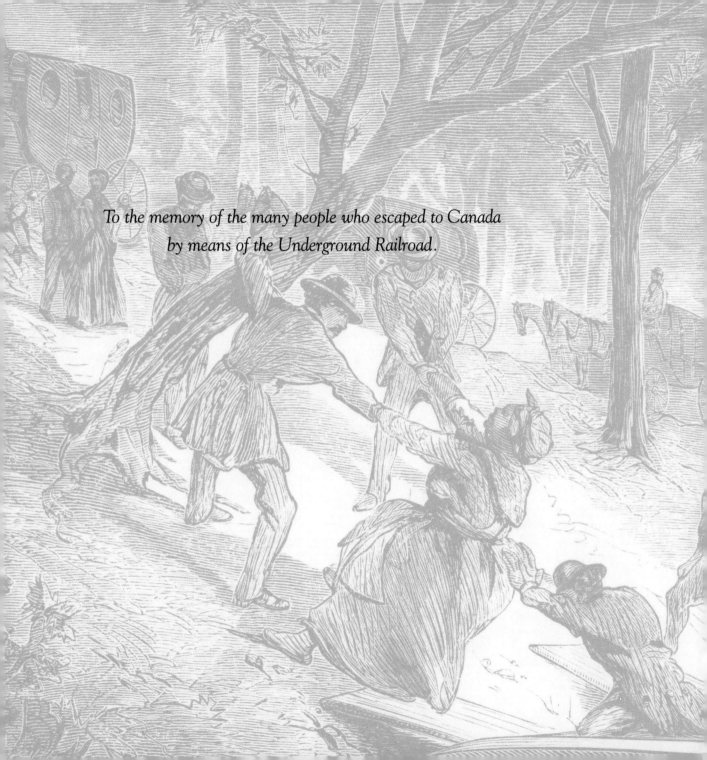

To the memory of the many people who escaped to Canada by means of the Underground Railroad.

CAUTION!!!

FROM information received from reliable sources, we learn that parties are at present in Toronto, endeavouring to induce colored persons to go to the States in their employ as servants. From the character of the propositions, there is reason to believe that "foul play" is intended. Possibly, that Constable Pope's designs on the fugitives and others are being carried out.

Individuals have proposed to women to go to Detroit to live in their service, and another party under circumstances of great suspicion, to a boy to go as far South as Philadelphia. We say to our people, lisen to no flattering proposals of the sort. You are in Canada, and let no misplaced confidence in this or the other smooth-tongued Yankee, or British subject either, who may be mercenary enough to ensnare you into bondage by collusion with kidnappers in the States, deprive you of your liberty...

An excerpt from the Provincial Freedman, *April 21, 1851.*

Table of Contents

Acknowledgements

This book is more than a labour of love. Many people have heard of the Underground Railroad that brought thousands of runaway slaves to freedom in Canada, but very few know that Toronto was an important terminus of those secret routes. Dr. Daniel Hill, President Emeritus of the Ontario Black History Society, wrote several pioneering articles on the history of Blacks in Toronto in addition to his well-known book, *The Freedom-Seekers: Blacks in Early Canada*. These earlier articles are known only to a small coterie of researchers and historians, but they and the work of a number of other earlier historians have been enormously important to our work. In the area of African Canadian history, we also recognize the important scholarship and contributions of Dr. James W. St.G. Walker and the role he has played as a mentor to us in our work over the years. *The Underground Railroad: Next Stop, Toronto!*, therefore, has enabled us to build on the ground-breaking work of Dr. Hill, Dr. Walker and others and to bring to the public something that we feel is not only important but which has also previously been largely unexplored. For that we feel immensely gratified.

As always, there are many fortuitous events that magically come together to give birth to the "baby." The information contained in this book was gathered over the course of a two-year research project that was part of the Historic Sites and Monuments Commission of Canada's initiative to recognize sites associated with the Underground Railroad. We take this opportunity to thank the Consultative Committee, including Rosemary Sadlier of the Ontario Black History Society, Daniel O'Brien of the Ontario Ministry of Culture, Christine Lockett of the ROM, Madge Logan and Catherine Slaney, as well as the Parks Canada staff members, who so ably steered the original project out of which our research for this book came. It is they who have generously permitted us to share the discoveries we made in the course of our research. In particular we are grateful to Ross Thompson, Southwestern Ontario, Field Unit Superintendent; Rob Watt, Project Manager; historians Owen Thomas and Shannon Ricketts; and curator Derek Cooke – all of Parks Canada – for their enthusiasm, dedication and hard work on We would also like to thank Tom Lackey for a great script, and Steve and Claudette Shaw of Steve Shaw Productions for their tireless effort and professionalism in producing in a very short time span "The Underground Railroad: Next Stop, Freedom!" This experiential theatre production, which made its debut at the Royal Ontario Museum in April 2002, was a fascinating project and we thoroughly enjoyed our work on it.

We are also very grateful to the numerous individuals and archival repositories for the use of their photographic and other visual materials: Dr. Daniel and Donna Hill, Pastor Michael Morris and Rochelle Williams, church historian, at the First Baptist Church, Toronto; Jill Delaney, Researcher Services Division and Martha Marleau, Art Acquisition and Research, National Archives of Canada; Donald Nethery, Museum and Archives, Toronto District School Board; Karen Teeple, City of Toronto Archives; Henri Pilon, Archivist, Trinity College Archives, University of Toronto. Alan Walker, Special Collections, Toronto Reference Library; Karen Jania, Access and Reference Services, Bentley Historical Library, University of Michigan; Owen Jenkins, Central Agencies, Transportation, Photographic Records and Documentary Art Portfolio, and Ralph Coram, Senior Archivist, Finance and Architectural Records Portfolio, Archives of Ontario, Toronto; Rob Medina, Chicago Historical Society and Gillian Small and Eleanor Peterson, the Ontario Black History Society. The images enhance tremendously the quality and appeal of the text.

Finally, we are indebted to Jane Gibson and Barry Penhale, the publishers at Natural Heritage Books, for their interest and dedication to ensuring that this work was brought to the public. Without their vision, the book might not have seen the light of day. We appreciate and thank them and Shannon MacMillan, assistant to the publisher, for their hard work and meticulous attention to detail. As always, we acknowledge and thank our families – Norm, Marjorie, Marishana, Alpha, Habiba, Lamarana and Akil – for their patience and unending support.

Foreword – Parks Canada

The Underground Railroad: Next Stop, Toronto! is an independently produced companion work to the Parks Canada experiential theatre exhibit, "The Underground Railroad: Next Stop, Freedom!" Although the exhibit evolved over a period of roughly two years, the background to the project spans almost two decades. Its origins stemmed from the groundbreaking work of Karolyn Smardz (one of the authors of this book) who rediscovered the fascinating story of Thornton and Lucie Blackburn. The Blackburns were people of colour who escaped slavery in the United States, came to Canada and, by the time of their deaths, had established themselves as highly successful entrepreneurs in the City of Toronto by owning the city's first cab business.

A submission was later made by the Ontario Black History Society to have the former homestead of Thornton and Lucie Blackburn recognized by the federal government as a National Historic Site. Now the location of the Toronto District School Board's Inglenook Community High School, the Blackburn residence has long since disappeared. This led the Historic Sites and Monuments Board of Canada (the body tasked with advising the Minister of Heritage whether a person, place, or event is of national importance) to recommend that Thornton and Lucie be commemorated as people of national significance.

Because the resulting designation did not include the former Blackburn homestead, the Historic Sites and Monuments Board of Canada (the HSMBC) also recommended that "... a presentation of the UGRR urban settlers should be developed and installed in a museum or other appropriate location in Toronto" with the aid of the Ontario Black History Society. The resulting exhibit was created in response to this Board recommendation. A consultative committee was formed consisting of a number of stakeholders and/or members of the Black community along with Parks Canada specialists, and through their tireless dedication and seemingly bottomless energy, the project gained much direction and focus. The Royal Ontario Museum also became a major partner and provided the space and important support through their educational programme.

"The Underground Railroad: Next Stop, Freedom!" provided the committee with an excellent opportunity to add important research to the study of African-Canadian Underground Railroad history and, also, to further explore the unique urban story of the UGRR in Toronto. The major work dealing with the Black urban UGRR experience is Daniel Hill's *The Freedom-Seekers: Blacks in Early Canada*, but it was published some twenty years ago. Since that time, much more information has been uncovered, adding a great deal of depth and context to this already compelling episode in Canadian history.

Adrienne Shadd, Afua Cooper and Karolyn Smardz Frost were recruited to aid with the collection of information for the project and the quality of the research they uncovered quickly proved that we were blessed with the best possible research team. However, it soon became evident that the project also needed a written supplement to the exhibit, one that would allow many of the themes that were only mentioned briefly in the production to be examined more fully. The research team came up with the idea of independently producing the supplement, a project that exhibition project manager Rob Watt and I wholeheartedly endorsed. Such was the genesis of *The Underground Railroad: Next Stop, Toronto!*

This publication increases the accessibility of "The Underground Railroad: Next Stop, Freedom!" by allowing those who are not able to attend the show a chance to join in the learning experience wherever they might be. Also, it provides some much-needed quality material which can be used in the schools, a point of extreme importance since education was identified as the primary aim of this project from a very early date. *The Underground Railroad: Next Stop, Toronto!* provides a tangible and well-written companion to the film exhibit that can be used either as a stand-alone resource or else to enhance the experience of the exhibit. My sincerest congratulations go to its authors.

Owen Thomas, Historian
Parks Canada, Ottawa

A Word From the Ontario Black History Society

The Underground Railroad, the freedom movement responsible for inspiring and/or transporting thousands of African Americans into more secure areas, has been steeped in myth and legend. This is partly because of the highly secret nature of this escape system and also due to the limited research that has been directed towards the 20,000 to 40,000 Black immigrants who made Canada their home. This book, *The Underground Railroad: Next Stop, Toronto!*, is a welcomed addition to a relatively brief list of African-Canadian historical works. It provides valuable information on the lives of a range of freedom seekers who made Canada, and Toronto, the final stop on their journey to freedom.

This resource illuminates the experiences and contributions of numerous Africans arriving from the United States via the Underground Railroad who settled in the Toronto area. It provides harrowing examples of their escape stories and startling examples of their lives in Toronto where they comprised at least 2,000 out of a population of 45,000 in the 1850s. It is difficult to determine the exact number of Black people in Toronto since some census data is unavailable, but even if it were available, everyone was not always included, and there were other discrepancies. Not only were African Americans cautioned not to tell much about where they came from or who assisted them (if anyone) in order to protect their Underground Railroad route and helpers, they also may have kept their racial/ethnic origins to themselves if their features allowed them to pass for people of European or even Native ancestry. This was felt to be necessary to rule out the possibility of potential re-enslavement.

Why Canada? Because it was largely English-speaking, it may have offered familiar destinations previously visited on travels with their owner, but primarily, if all other means of transportation were blocked, they could still walk here. Why Canada? Because by 1834, the effective date of the British Imperial Act, Canada was clearly an anti-slavery country where the mere touching of British soil made one free.

Why Toronto? If the entire country were open to potential freedom seekers, why would they choose to come to Toronto? Toronto was the business and cultural capital of the country. Self-sufficiency was possible because there were plenty of jobs. It was also a major centre of abolitionist thought and activity – Toronto was the safest city in the safest country. This is further supported by the fact that the Convention of Colored Freemen took place there.

While notables such as Mary Ann Shadd, Harriet Tubman, Henry Bibb and Dr. Anderson Abbott are included, so too are the stories of lesser-known people from Thornton and Lucie Blackburn, nominated by the Ontario Black History Society as nationally historic, through to Deborah Brown. Recently Deborah Brown became the subject and "narrator" of an Ontario Black History Society-initiated experiential theatre exhibition, created with support from Parks Canada and on exhibit at the Royal Ontario Museum in Toronto.

In addition to several escape/survival stories are accounts of early life in Toronto. The challenges of travelling into the downtown core from the rural farming communities of outlying areas like the Township of York, the backbreaking nature of the work available to newcomers, and the high mortality rate among infants and young people because of fevers, infections, cholera, consumption and even teething were part of their daily life. One learns that Blacks, although now free of enslavement, were affected by numerous other problems.

Unlike many parts of the province, schools and institutions of higher learning were always open to Blacks in Toronto. However, mainstream organizations and institutions did not provide the same level of acceptance or meet the needs of the African-Canadian population. Churches, cultural organizations and aid societies developed to facilitate the settlement of new arrivals. The Black community created institutions to serve their community and worked co-operatively with white abolitionists to create the Anti-Slavery Society of Canada.

One Underground Railroad myth suggests that there were no Black people in Canada until the 1850s. This book outlines the very early presence of Blacks in Toronto and the nature of their contribution to the development of Canada from their participation as soldiers and road builders through to business owners, labourers and professionals. Then, as now, African Canadians were represented in every level of society.

This book, like the Ontario Black History Society's project to create a museum of African-Canadian history in Toronto, is an important contribution ensuring that African-Canadian stories, experiences and achievements are widely appreciated and understood in support of today's truths and tomorrow's dreams.

Rosemary Sadlier, President
Ontario Black History Society

Introduction

Slavery existed in North America almost from the time of the first European settlement on the continent. At first, it was Native people who were bound to unwilling and unpaid labour, but soon the French and British sought new resources. Beginning in 1619, when the first slave ship landed a cargo of Black men and women at Jamestown, Virginia, millions of people were stolen from their homes in Africa to be sold to the American market. They were shipped across the ocean and brought to work in the fields and farms, mines, homes and early business establishments in what is now the United States and Canada. After the American Revolution, most of the Northern U.S. states began to see the contradiction between depending upon this unpaid labour system and the freedom promised in the new American Constitution. By 1800, some Northern states and Upper Canada (what is now Ontario) had moved towards the abolition of slavery. However, the institution of slavery continued to provide the basis of the prosperity for the largely agricultural economy of the states of the American South.

The colored people in Toronto are, on the whole, remarkably industrious. Their condition is such as to gratify the philanthropist, and afford encouragement to the friends of emancipation everywhere. A portion of them sustain a lyceum or debating club (which is attended by both sexes) where debates are held, and original essays read. A large majority of the adult colored people are refugees from the South ...[1]

Many people thought slavery was wrong. Some religious groups, such as the Society of Friends (known as the Quakers), preached against enslaving other people.

Beginning late in the 18th century, in England, the United States and Canada, individuals called "abolitionists" stood forth to oppose slavery. They established anti-slavery organizations, published pamphlets and books, gave public lectures and pressured their political representatives to try to have slavery made illegal. But the system of slavery was very profitable, and many people in the Northern states would not accept even free African Americans as equal citizens with them. Many laws were passed to prevent Black Americans from gaining an education, participating in the political process, or even from deciding where they could live and work. Over time, Southerners who supported slavery came to pretend that African Americans could not take care of themselves if they were not slaves, and so slavery itself came to be seen by some people as beneficial. But this was a lie to serve the financial interests of wealthy slaveholders.

After Britain ended slavery throughout her Empire, by an act passed in 1833, the provinces of Canada – especially Upper Canada – became the principal destination of fugitive slaves. The reasons for this are discussed later in this volume. Many former slaves, mostly those who had lived on farms and plantations in the United States, wanted to purchase their own farmland and live independently. Rural colonies of fugitive slaves such as the Wilberforce Settlement north of London, the Elgin Settlement at Buxton, the Oro Settlement above Lake Simcoe and the Refugee Home Society near Windsor were testimony to the deep desire of Black pioneers in Upper Canada to own and operate their own farms and govern their own communities. However, other people who had lived in the urban centres of the Southern and Northern United States had skills and abilities best suited to city life. They found employment, opened businesses, and established a rich and complex community right in the heart of what is now Canada's largest city, Toronto. And so the title for this book, *The Underground Railroad: Next Stop, Toronto!*

Most people do not think of the City of Toronto as a major terminus of the Underground Railroad. Yet before the outbreak of the Civil War ended slavery in the United States in 1865, more than 2,000 Black people had settled in the downtown core of the city and on the outskirts of the growing urban centre. There they developed a rich and complex "world-within-a-world," served by active social, intellectual, political, charitable and religious institutions and organizations.

When fugitive slaves arrived in York (Toronto), they found a very different city from the one that we know today. Most houses and stores were built of wood, although there were wealthy people's homes, and large and impressive public buildings built of fine red brick. The principal shopping and business district spread out east and west along King Street on either side of Yonge. There were only a few residential streets north of Queen. The area between Dundas Street and Bloor, the city limits, was farmland and bush, interspersed with large estates.

African-Canadian Toronto included the descendants of former slaves of British and United Empire Loyalist settlers, and some people from the West Indies, but by far the largest proportion of the Black population at mid-century were immigrants from the United States. The majority were fugitive slaves who sought a new home and a new life in freedom. These were joined by educated and propertied free Black families from both the North and the South, especially after 1850 when their continued liberty in their American home was threatened by the passage of the Fugitive Slave Act.[2]

Deborah Brown, a fugitive slave woman, was one of the many who came to Toronto via the Underground Railroad.
From John Ross Robertson, *Landmarks of Toronto*, Volume 6 (Toronto: J. Ross Robertson, 1914) 46.

I Deborah Brown: A Fugitive Slave Woman

On December 8, 1908, *The Evening Telegram* featured an elderly woman named Deborah Brown in a story on the old Seaton Village community. Mrs. Brown had died in 1898 and is reported to have been 111 years old at the time of her death. She was considered to be the oldest resident in Seaton Village and her house was said to be the oldest building in the village. Deborah Brown was a former slave from Maryland, United States. She had escaped to Canada in the mid-1800s with her husband, Perry, when they learned he was to be sold. The couple moved to the Township of York, north of Bloor Street, the northern boundary of the City of Toronto at the time. They lived in the same one-storey frame cottage on Markham Street near Bathurst and Bloor for over 50 years.

Nowadays it is hard for us to imagine that when Deborah and Perry Brown first moved to the area it was rural farmland. During the 1870s, their neighbourhood, by then known as Seaton Village, was bounded by Bedford Road on the east, Christie Street on the west, and Davenport Road to the north, with Bloor Street as its southern perimeter. In 1888, Seaton Village and the Town of Yorkville, which had developed just to the east around Yonge and Bloor streets, were annexed to the growing City of Toronto. In a span of fifty years, the region where the Browns lived had gone from being on the rural fringes to being in the centre of the city.

Deborah Brown worked as a washerwoman, and her husband was a labourer. The Browns were a working-class family judging from their occupations and their standard of living. Deborah Brown could not read or write and her husband Perry was

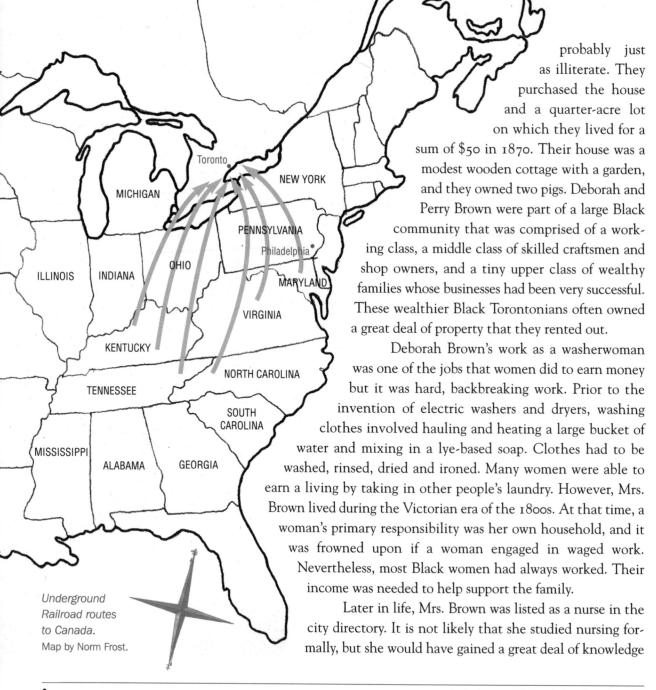

MICHIGAN

Toronto

NEW YORK

PENNSYLVANIA

Philadelphia

ILLINOIS INDIANA OHIO

MARYLAND

VIRGINIA

KENTUCKY

NORTH CAROLINA

TENNESSEE

SOUTH CAROLINA

MISSISSIPPI ALABAMA GEORGIA

Underground Railroad routes to Canada.
Map by Norm Frost.

probably just as illiterate. They purchased the house and a quarter-acre lot on which they lived for a sum of $50 in 1870. Their house was a modest wooden cottage with a garden, and they owned two pigs. Deborah and Perry Brown were part of a large Black community that was comprised of a working class, a middle class of skilled craftsmen and shop owners, and a tiny upper class of wealthy families whose businesses had been very successful. These wealthier Black Torontonians often owned a great deal of property that they rented out.

Deborah Brown's work as a washerwoman was one of the jobs that women did to earn money but it was hard, backbreaking work. Prior to the invention of electric washers and dryers, washing clothes involved hauling and heating a large bucket of water and mixing in a lye-based soap. Clothes had to be washed, rinsed, dried and ironed. Many women were able to earn a living by taking in other people's laundry. However, Mrs. Brown lived during the Victorian era of the 1800s. At that time, a woman's primary responsibility was her own household, and it was frowned upon if a woman engaged in waged work. Nevertheless, most Black women had always worked. Their income was needed to help support the family.

Later in life, Mrs. Brown was listed as a nurse in the city directory. It is not likely that she studied nursing formally, but she would have gained a great deal of knowledge

Deborah Brown's cottage at 691 Markham Street, the oldest house in Seaton Village, is the one illustrated here. From *Landmarks of Toronto*, Volume 6, 43. Courtesy of Toronto Reference Library.

over the years in curing various sicknesses through the use of herbs, roots and the like. It would not have been unusual for her to apply her considerable experience and know-how to nurse family and friends back to health.

The Browns were of the Wesleyan Methodist faith. They probably attended the Black churches in downtown Toronto from time to time – certainly on special occasions like Christmas, Easter and Emancipation Day, the time set aside in early August to celebrate the British Act of Parliament of 1833 that freed slaves throughout the British Empire. However, Deborah Brown also attended the Methodist church in Seaton Village. *The Evening Telegram* article noted that even in extreme old age Mrs. Brown continued to be a member of the Sunday School, and delighted in getting up on the platform with the children at Sunday School anniversary celebrations. Most Black people at that time belonged to either the Methodist or Baptist faith.

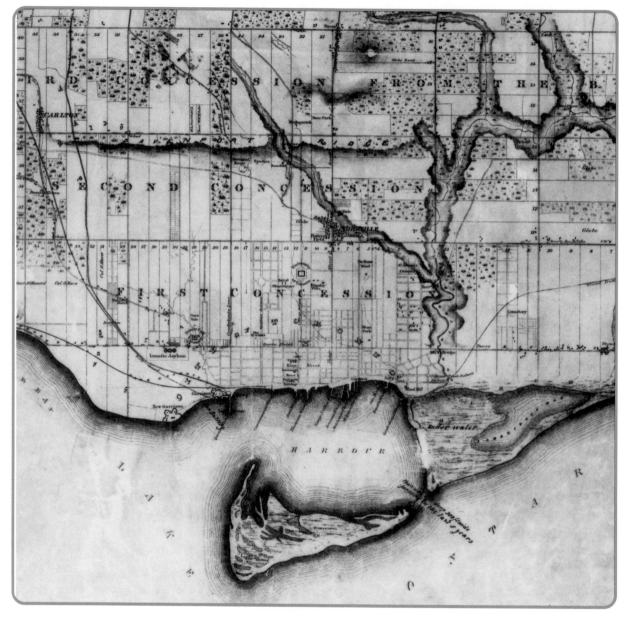

Map of Township of York, 1852. Courtesy of National Archives of Canada NMC 26683.

Deborah Brown had at least one child that we know of, Sarah Brooks. An eight-year-old child named William H. Brown, born in the United States, lived with Deborah and Perry in 1861. But because of Deborah's age of 56, it is not certain whether William was her child or grandchild. He may even have been a nephew or great nephew. Unfortunately, after 1861, William was not listed in the same household as Deborah Brown again, and we are not sure what happened to him.

More is known about daughter Sarah, however. She was born in the United States and she in turn had a daughter named Amelia, who was also American-born. According to the census records of the time, it is known that these women were living on Centre Street in St. John's Ward. Sarah was 56 and Amelia was 23 years of age in 1881. Both were widows. Like Deborah, they too worked as laundresses. We think that Sarah Brooks did not come to Canada with her parents, and that she may have been left behind in slavery.

Rather than making a "return trip" south after the Civil War, some African Canadians brought their family members north to live with them in Canada after the Emancipation Proclamation. On January 1, 1863, Abraham Lincoln, President of the United States, freed the American slaves in the states that had rebelled against the Union.

York (Toronto), capital of Upper Canada, *1803. Edward Walsh, artist.* Courtesy of Toronto Culture Division, Market Gallery Art Collection.

2 Blacks in Early Toronto

Blacks helped lay the foundation for the town of York, as Toronto was first named, right from its beginning as an important colonial town in 1793. Initially the area, situated in a sheltered harbour on the banks of Lake Ontario, was the site of a French fort and a centre for fur traders. In 1793, when the new Lieutenant-Governor of Upper Canada (later Ontario) John Graves Simcoe arrived, he decided to establish York as a defence town. This Simcoe believed was necessary, as Canada had just come out of a war with the United States, and the defence of the British colony was of the highest priority. By 1799, there were about 25 Blacks living in the town out of a population of about 200. In this very early period, Blacks chopped down trees, helped to clear the forest, constructed buildings, built roads, served in the army and worked in the homes of other settlers.

> ### The Long Family
> One free family was the Long family. This family, headed by Loyalist pioneer Peter Long, originally came from Massachusetts. Long served as a gunner for the British forces during the Revolutionary war, on a ship named the Nova Scotia. After the war ended in 1783, Long settled in New Brunswick, but moved his family of ten to York [Toronto] in 1793 and settled in the Don Valley area. Long established a large farm in the Don Valley and sold his produce in the markets of York. Two of his sons served in the Upper Canadian militia during the Rebellion of 1837.

Blacks in York came from diverse backgrounds and origins. There were those of Loyalist background, and there were both free Blacks and slaves within this population. There were African-American fugitive slaves. Some free African Americans

Detail from Toronto from the Upper Don River, *1855. Mary Hasting Meyer, artist.* Courtesy of Toronto Culture Division, Market Gallery Art Collection.

made York their home during this early period. As well, sprinklings of Caribbean Blacks existed within this pioneering population.

Free Blacks were among the early road builders of York and the rest of the province. In 1799, several Black men won the contract to build a road from Davenport Road to Castle Frank Road, just west of the Don River.[1] This road was instrumental in linking the east and west ends of the town.

It should be noted that several important persons like Peter Russell, Administrator of Upper Canada following the departure of Simcoe, were slaveholders. William Jarvis, the first Sheriff of York, also owned slaves. Slavery was not officially abolished in York and Upper Canada until after the British government's 1833 Emancipation Act took effect, freeing all the slaves owned by British subjects around the world, most notably in the West Indies and Canada.

Pompadour Family

In contrast to the Long family, the wife and the children of Pompadour, a free Black, were the slaves of Peter Russell and his sister Elizabeth. Russell became the Provincial Administrator after Simcoe's departure from Canada. The family consisted of Peggy, the mother, three children – Jupiter, Milly, and Amy – and the father known as Mr. Pompadour, who worked for the Russell family for wages. Peggy and her children were the Russells' house slaves. However, they sometimes also worked on the Russell farm located at Queen and Peter streets.

Peggy hated slavery and several times tried to run away from the Russells. On one such occasion, Peter Russell responded by having Peggy jailed. In 1803, Russell wrote to Matthew Elliot, a Loyalist slaveholder living at Amherstburg near Windsor. Elliot had promised to buy Peggy from Russell but seemed to have reneged on his promise. In the letter, Russell stated that after paying the jailer 10 pounds to have Peggy released from jail, she had disappeared. He also stated that his sister Elizabeth would not permit her to enter the house. Russell was anxious to sell Peggy, whom he described as "very troublesome," to Elliot.

However, Peggy remained with the Russells and continued being their slave. The fact that she was an adult woman, and Peter Russell called her "Peggy," and the fact that he did not use her last name, indicated her low status as a slave. However by 1806, Peter Russell placed an advertisement in the Upper Canada Gazette *offering Peggy and her son Jupiter for sale.*

The advertisement provides an insight into the nature of the work done by enslaved people in York. Peggy cooked and washed for the Russells, and also undertook crucial tasks like soap and candle-making, work that was essential for pioneering life. Most likely her daughters, Milly and Amy, performed the same kinds of household duties. The boy, Jupiter, worked as a farm labourer, but also spent time as a house slave. Their daily responsibilities demonstrate that, not only did they contribute to making other people's lives comfortable, but they also helped in the building of a new society.

Peter Russell died in 1808 and passed on all his property, including the slaves, to his sister Elizabeth. She gave Amy as a "gift" to her goddaughter Elizabeth Denison. Reverend Henry

> ## TO BE SOLD,
> ### A BLACK WOMAN, named
> PEGGY, aged about forty years ; and a Black boy her son, named JUPITER, aged about fifteen years, both of them the property of the Subscriber.
>
> The Woman is a tolerable Cook and washer woman and perfectly understands making Soap and Candles.
>
> The Boy is tall and strong of his age, and has been employed in Country business, but brought up principally as a House Servant—They are each of them Servants for life. The Price for the Wowan is one hundred and fifty Dollars—for the Boy two hundred Dollars, payable in three years with Interest from the day of Sale and to be properly secured by Bond &c.—But one fourth less will be taken in ready Money.
>
> PETER RUSSELL.
>
> York, Feb. 10th 1806.

Peter Russell advertised Peggy and her son Jupiter Pompadour for sale on February 22, 1806. From Upper Canada Gazette, *Volume XV, Number 45.*

Scadding, in his history of early Toronto, entitled Toronto of Old, *notes that Amy Pompadour was one of several Blacks that people used to see around town when it was still called York. Scadding described her as a "tall, comely, Negress...of servile descent" who, in the days when slavery was just dying out in Upper Canada, was quite a curiosity because of her slave status. It is not known what subsequently happened to Peggy, the rest of her children, or her husband, Pompadour.*

But life in York was changing – and so, too, for Black people. The War of 1812[2] led to an increase in the overall population of the province and Toronto. The War was fought between Britain and the United States, over the ownership of Canada. York (Toronto) was temporarily occupied by the Americans. Many Black men from York and the rest of the province fought in the British army and militias in defence of Upper Canada. After this war, more and more Black people from the United States began to filter into Upper Canada. They heard that any slave reaching British soil would be set free.

By 1828, the Black population in the city had grown in size and Blacks were now establishing themselves in several professions. One African Torontonian for whom there is some information is John Y. Butler, a barber, who opened a salon in 1825. It is reported that Butler became very successful at his job, so much so that, by 1827, he was employing white men and women as house servants and babysitters. William Lyon Mackenzie, reformer, politician, and newspaper publisher, mentioned this fact in his paper, the *Colonial Advocate* on October 4, 1827.

Advertisement for Moses Holmes' hairdressing establishment. From the Colonial Advocate, *September 29, 1831 (Toronto, U. C.), weekly [L 23/ N 8, reel 2].*

MOSES HOLMES,

FASHIONABLE HAIR CUTTER AND EASY SHAVER.

King Street.

RESPECTFULLY informs the Gentlemen of York, that he has commenced business as a Hair Dresser in that central shop west of the market square lately occupied by Mr. Mills the Hatter, where he solicits a share of public patronage, which he will endeavour to merit by the utmost attention to his customers.

A newspaper ad promotes another Black Toronto barber by the name of Moses Holmes. He originally came from Virginia and was a free man. The ad appeared in the *Colonial Advocate* in 1837.

The couple that established the first cab company in Toronto, Thornton and Lucie Blackburn, arrived in the city in 1834. That year the name "York" was changed back to "Toronto," the original Native name for the area.

By this date, the population was around nine thousand, with at least 400 Blacks. The foundations were being laid for the building of significant community institutions such as businesses, churches, social reform societies, schools and political organizations. By the middle of the century, many African Americans had found lives and new homes in the city. Perhaps the best description of what life was like for Black immigrants comes from a report from the *New York Tribune* reprinted in the April 1, 1858 edition of the *Anti-Slavery Reporter* and entitled "The Negroes of Toronto":

"The large and thriving city of Toronto contains a more numerous coloured population than any other town of Canada. Out of its 50,000 inhabitants, from 1200 to 1600 are estimated to be coloured. Though the great majority belong to the class of unskilled labourers, among them are to be found followers of a great number and variety of occupations. One of them, a man of wealth, lives upon his means…one is a regularly educated physician; three are studying law; one medicine; two at least are master builders, taking contracts, and employing a number of journeymen, both white and black; four are grocers, and the store of one of them – the only one we visited was in a good part of the town, handsome, neat well-stocked and evidently doing a thriving business, the customers being mostly whites; one keeps a large livery-stable, one of the best in town, and is employed to take the mails to and from the post office to the railroad depots, steamboats & c.; several within the precincts of the city are occupied in farming and gardening; others are bricklayers, carpenters, shoemakers, plasterers, blacksmiths, and carters. Many find employment in sawing and chopping the wood, which is the general fuel; and the barbers and waiters in hotels and private families are almost exclusively coloured men…many of them have accumulated considerable property (especially) among the older residents [in] real estate…."

"Heavy weights – Arrival of a Party at League Island." (Fifteen escaped in this schooner.) From William Still, *The Underground Rail Road* (Philadelphia: Porter & Coates, 1872) Opp. 561. (TRL).
Toronto Public Library, Special Collections, Genealogy & Maps Centre.

3 Underground Railroad to Toronto

In March 1793, an enslaved woman named Chloe Cooley was bound and transported from the Niagara Region to the United States by her owner, William Fromond (or Vrooman). Although Cooley had screamed and resisted violently, there was nothing that the Executive Council of Upper Canada could do because she was legally a slave. Her owner was perfectly within his rights to sell her in the United States (or anywhere else for that matter). She was his property and could be bought and sold like any of his other personal belongings.

The new Lieutenant-Governor of Upper Canada, John Graves Simcoe, who had just arrived in 1793, was a staunch abolitionist. Despite opposition among the slave-holding members of the legislature, he moved to pass a bill that same year banning the importation of slaves into the province. Although the new Act of the Upper Canadian parliament did not free any slaves outright, it did allow for the eventual emancipation of the children of slaves. They would be "free" upon reaching the age of 25 years.

What this did was to set the stage for the influx of thousands of escaped slaves from the American South. By the early 1800s, secret routes were being used by slaves to escape to the North and Canada. Many of these routes were old Indian or military trails. Gradually a more organized system of assisting fugitive slaves evolved. This became known as the "Underground Railroad." At the peak of its activity, this "railroad" in the 1850s consisted of half-a-dozen major routes and numerous secondary routes leading from the southern United States to Canada, Mexico and the Caribbean.

Chapter VII.

An act to prevent the further introduction of slaves, and to limit the term of contracts for servitude within this province.

[Passed July 9, 1793.]

WHEREAS it is unjust that a people who enjoy freedom by law should encourage the introduction of slaves, and whereas it is highly expedient to abolish slavery in this province, so far as the same may gradually be done without violating private property; be it enacted by the King's most excellent Majesty, by and with the advice and consent of the legislative council and assembly of the province of Upper Canada, constituted and assembled by virtue of and under the authority of an act passed in the parliament of Great Britain, entitled, "An act to repeal certain parts of an act passed in the fourteenth year of his Majesty's reign, entitled, 'An act for making more effectual provision for the government of the province of Quebec, in North America, and to make further provision for the government of the said province,'" and by the authority of the same, That from and after the passing of this act, so much of a certain act of the parliament of Great Britain, passed in the thirtieth year of his present Majesty, entitled, "An act for encouraging new settlers in his Majesty's colonies and plantations in America," as may enable the governor or lieutenant governor of this province, heretofore parcel of his Majesty's province of Quebec, to grant a license for importing into the same any negro or negroes, shall be, and the same is hereby repealed; and that from and after the passing of this act, it shall not be lawful for the governor, lieutenant governor, or person administering the government of this province, to grant a license for the importation of any negro or other person to be subjected to the condition of a slave, or to a bounden involuntary service for life, into any part of this province; nor shall any negro, or other person who shall come or be brought into this province after the passing of this act, be subject to the condition of a slave, or to such service as aforesaid, within this province, nor shall any voluntary contract of service or indentures that may be entered into by any parties within this province, after the passing of this act, be binding on them or either of them for a longer time than a term of nine years, from the day of the date of such contract.

Excerpt from the parliamentary act to limit slavery as initiated in 1793 by Lieutenant-Governor John Graves Simcoe.
Courtesy of the Ontario Black History Society.

The Underground Railroad was not a real railroad. It referred to the system of secret routes and safe houses by which escaped slaves made their way north to freedom. Wilbur Siebert in *The Underground Railroad from Slavery to Freedom* tells us that the term originated in 1831 when a fugitive slave from Kentucky, Tice Davids, escaped across the Ohio River and disappeared. Davids' master, who had been in hot pursuit, watched as his property swam across the river. Once the slave reached the shore, however, he could not be found. After a lengthy search, Davids' owner remarked, "The d — d Abolitionists must have a rail road under the ground by which they run off n —."[1]

Because steam locomotion was a new form of transportation, the name "Underground Railroad" caught on and was used by abolitionists as a metaphor to

Escaping with Master's Carriages and Horses. Harriet Shephard, and her five children, with five other passengers. From William Still, *The Underground Rail Road* (1872) 302. Toronto Public Library (TRL), Special Collections, Genealogy & Maps Centre.

describe their activities in assisting escaping slaves. This railroad terminology included "stations" or "stops," houses in which sympathizers took in fugitives temporarily, "stationmasters" or the selfless people who took them in and "conductors" who risked their own lives in transporting runaways from one point to the next. "Cargo" was the human "freight" that risked all for their very freedom. The Underground Railroad involved many people of good will, all willing to take risks, including Blacks, Whites and Native Americans. These courageous people provided shelter, food, clothing and secrecy to assist escaping slaves. Sometimes "conductors" drove wagons, carriages or carts with slaves hidden in false compartments. At other times, fugitives were disguised as the slaves driving their "owners," who in reality were Underground Railroad workers. Sometimes they were dressed in fancy clothing,

Harriet Tubman (1823-1913) was the fugitive Maryland slave who led more than 300 slaves to freedom on the Underground Railroad. Known as the "Moses of Her People," she served the Union Army as a nurse, scout and a spy during the Civil War. Library of Congress.

women dressed up as men and men as women, and those who were light-skinned disguised themselves as white people or even slave owners. Husband and wife fugitives, William and Ellen Craft, were able to win their freedom by disguising themselves as slave and master because of Ellen's light skin and male costume. There were numerous cases of fugitives hiding in crates and being shipped north by rail, such as Henry "Box" Brown who acquired his middle name as a result of having escaped this way. A number of people risked their lives by making trips into the south to emancipate loved ones from the jaws of slavery.

Perhaps the best-known Underground Railroad "conductor" was Harriet Tubman. This incredible woman is believed to have returned nineteen times to the Southern States, where slavery was a part of everyday life, to rescue approximately 300 people. Harriet Tubman was herself an escaped slave from Maryland. From 1851 to 1857, she made St. Catharines, Canada West,[2] her base of operations. She was never caught, although she was a wanted fugitive with a considerable bounty on her head. As Harriet once exclaimed, "I never ran my train off the track, and I never lost a passenger."

African Americans had been coming to Canada for decades, but it was the passage of the dreaded Fugitive Slave Act of 1850 that sent many thousands more fleeing across the

border. This Act required officials to arrest and detain any person suspected of being a runaway slave and rewarded those who did. Free Blacks as well as fugitives were sometimes kidnapped and sent into slavery. As a result, thousands of African Americans living in freedom in the northern American states packed up and fled to Canada. In effect, no Black, living in the United States, slave or free, was safe from the slave catcher after the passage of this law.

The vast majority of escaping slaves were men – about 80 percent. It was far more difficult for women who were pregnant or with families of young children to make the dangerous trip north. At first, fugitives came on foot, by boat, in covered wagons and carriages and, by the 1850s, on trains in hidden compartments.

Escape by boat was one of the earliest and most widely used methods of entry, particularly for those living near the coast or along inland rivers. On the Great Lakes the boat service was extensive. Friendly captains leaving port cities such as Racine (Wisconsin); Chicago (Illinois); Detroit (Michigan); Sandusky, Cleveland and

One of the most important crossing places for fugitive slaves was from the Michigan shore to the area of what now is Windsor, Ontario. The City of Detroit is in the background.
Courtesy of Bentley Historical Library, University of Michigan.

Another means of escape was by horse-drawn vehicles.
Courtesy of City of Toronto Archives, TTC Fonds Series 71, Item 10180.

Toledo (Ohio) and Buffalo (New York) dropped off fugitives at ports in Canada West such as Windsor, Amherstburg, Owen Sound, Collingwood, Niagara Falls, St. Catharines, Hamilton, Toronto and Kingston. Blacks could remain in these towns or move further inland.

Some came to Toronto by reaching Montreal or Kingston first, either through the St. Lawrence River route or overland via the New England states. Toronto was then a relatively short boat trip away. Another common route was along the eastern seaboard of the United States, through the Niagara Region and across Lake Ontario to Toronto. Steamers and stagecoaches arrived and departed daily to and from Toronto, and many fugitives took the opportunity to use these methods of transportation. Regular travel by rail within Canada West did not begin until 1853 when the first rail line was built between Toronto and Lake Simcoe in that year. As more railways were built, fugitives could then escape into Canada by train from departure points in the United States.

Frank Wanzer, Emily Foster, Barnaby and Mary Elizabeth Grigsby making their bid for freedom. From William Still, *The Underground Rail Road* (1872) Opp. 125. Toronto Public Library, Special Collections, Genealogy & Maps Centre.

Wanzer and Grigsby Couples' Escape

Two couples who made a trip on the Underground Railroad were immortalized in the classic work, The Underground Rail Road, *written by Black abolitionist William Still in 1872. According to Still, Frank Wanzer and Emily Foster (alias Robert Scott and Ann Wood) and Barnaby and Mary Elizabeth Grigsby (alias John and Mary Boyer) escaped from Virginia on Christmas Eve, 1855, in a carriage owned by their masters. There were two men who escaped with them on horseback. The group left during the Christmas holiday because it would give them a couple of days extra time before their owners would realize they were missing.*

After travelling for 100 miles or so they were met by six white men and a boy who demanded to know where they were going. Realizing that they were runaway slaves, the white men ordered them to surrender. It was at this point that both the Black men and the women drew guns and knives and stood their ground. "Shoot! Shoot!! Shoot!!!" exclaimed one of the women, a pistol in one hand and a long dagger in the other, the fiery determination visible in her eyes. When the would-be slave catchers realized that they might not make it out alive, they moved aside and let the couples go on their way. However, the white posse managed to capture the two fugitives on horseback.

All of the escaped slaves were young – in their early twenties. The two women were sisters on the same plantation. Frank Wanzer and Barnaby Grigsby were slaves on nearby farms. None had been particularly well-treated by their masters.

The two couples made it to Philadelphia, in the free state of Pennsylvania. There they were taken in and cared for by members of the Philadelphia Vigilance Committee. This was one of many groups of Underground Railroad activists that assisted fugitive slaves in eluding the slave catchers. After recuperating in Philadelphia, the couples were sent on to Syracuse, New York, and the Underground Railroad 'stationmaster' Jermain Loguen, a Black minister there.

Frank Wanzer and Emily Foster, who were engaged, decided to tie the knot. Reverend Loguen performed the marriage ceremony. From there the couples went on to Toronto. Mrs. Agnes Willis, treasurer of the Toronto Ladies' Association for the Relief of Destitute Colored Fugitives, met with them and assisted them in obtaining employment. Mrs. Willis wrote a letter back to William Still of the Philadelphia Vigilance Committee as follows:

Toronto, 28th January, Monday evening, 1856

Mr. Still, Dear Sir: –
… They are all of them in pretty good spirits, and I have not doubt they will succeed in whatever business they take up. In the mean time the men are chopping wood and the ladies are getting plenty sewing. We are always glad to see our colored refugees safe here. I remain, dear sir, yours respectfully,

Agnes Willis
Treasurer to the Ladies' Society to aid colored refugees.

A portrait of William Still engraved by John Sartain of Philadelphia. From William Still, *Underground Rail Road Records*, Revised Edition, (Philadelphia: William , 1883) Frontispiece. Courtesy of the Ontario Black History Society.

When U.S. President Abraham Lincoln freed the slaves at the end of the Civil War, travel on the Underground Railroad halted. African Americans were liberated of their shackles and forged new lives in freedom. However, at least 30,000 to 40,000 people who took their passage on the Underground Railroad to Canada, had paved the way for their brothers and sisters in the United States. How did they fare in this new frontier? It is to the Black pioneers who settled in Toronto that we now turn.

British Methodist Episcopal (BME) Church on the west side of Chestnut Street, between Armoury and Dundas streets, June 1953. Courtesy of Toronto Public Library (TPL), J.V. Salmon Collection: S1-960.

4 Social, Cultural and Religious Life in Toronto's Black Community

African Torontonians were instrumental in establishing some of the earliest social, cultural and religious institutions in the city. Reform societies, educational associations, early personal insurance organizations, and those groups devoted to helping fugitive slaves and the poor of the city, proliferated. The Society for the Protection of Refugees, the Ladies Colored Fugitive Association, the Queen Victoria Benevolent Society (QVBS), and the Ladies Freedman's Aid Society were all founded by the Black women of the city.

Ellen Toyer Abbott led the Queen Victoria Benevolent Society. She was the wife of Wilson Ruffin Abbott, a very wealthy Black Torontonian, and mother of the first Black medical doctor to be born in Canada, Anderson Ruffin Abbott. The QVBS provided assistance to women in need, and helped with education, settling into the city and with burial requirements. The Ladies Colored Fugitive Association assisted runaway slaves in finding housing, jobs and generally establishing themselves in the city.

Black Torontonians founded some of the earliest churches in the city. The First Baptist Church has the distinction of being Toronto's oldest Black institution and the city's very first Baptist Assembly, begun in 1826 when 15 fugitive slaves met in worship on the shores of Lake Ontario. The First Baptist Church had its building at the corners of Queen and Victoria streets (at the present site of St. Michael's Hospital. Reverend Washington Christian pastored the congregation. This church emerged as a leading centre of Black abolitionist activity. It sponsored anti-slavery lectures, and

Emancipation Day in Toronto

Black Christians played a leading role in the annual Emancipation Day celebrations held in the city August First. This celebration commemorated the Emancipation Act of 1833 which ended slavery throughout the British slaveholding world, most notably the West Indies and Canada. African Torontonians saw and celebrated this event as the most important social event of the year. They began celebrating Emancipation Day as early as 1839, if not before. The event was marked by church services, picnics, marches and parades.

Jehu Jones, a Lutheran minister from Philadelphia, visited Toronto in 1839 and witnessed and participated in an Emancipation Day celebration. Jones wrote to New York newspaper editor, Charles B. Ray, informing Ray that the Toronto Abolition Society, a Black anti-slavery group, had organized that year's celebrations. It was this group that had extended an invitation to Jones.

Jones revealed that he attended a church service at the African Methodist Episcopal chapel, where Reverend Edward Miller delivered a sermon. From the chapel the celebrants joined a procession that marched to City Hall. Here, such city luminaries as the mayor, and anti-slavery leaders like the Reverend Grassett of the Anglican Church, gave speeches. Afterwards, the procession continued to the Commercial Hotel on Front Street, where celebrants "sat down to a superb dinner." More speeches were made at this dinner. Speakers toasted Queen Victoria and the Royal family praising them for their benevolence in abolishing slavery. The British flag flew everywhere. Jones ended the day by attending a tea party organized "by the ladies of Toronto" in honour of the event. Jones also commented that the parade was well-organized and controlled by Black marshals. The event was attended by Black and white, young, old and middle-aged, and he noted the co-operation across all levels of Black society, the various cultural institutions and the different religious denominations.

Dr. Anderson Ruffin Abbott also witnessed and participated in an Emancipation Day celebration in the 1850s, some fifteen or so years later. He, too, recorded his observations:

> … they provided a banquet which was held under a pavilion erected on a vacant lot running from Elizabeth Street to Sayre Street opposite Osgoode Hall, which was then a barracks for the 92nd West India Regiment. The procession was headed by the band of the Regiment. The tallest man in this Regiment was a Black man, a drummer, known as Black Charlie. The procession carried a Union Jack and a silk blue banner on which was inscribed in gilt letters "The Abolition Society, Organized 1844." The mayor of the city, Mr. Metcalfe, made a speech … followed by several other speeches of prominent citizens. These celebrations were carried on yearly amid much enthusiasm …."

Toronto's history with Emancipation Day continued into the twentieth century. In the 1920s, B. J. Spencer Pitt masterminded what became the Port Dalhousie Picnic or "Big Picnic" when Toronto's Black community took the ferry across Lake Ontario to Port Dalhousie, Ontario, a resort town near St. Catharines. In its heyday, the Big Picnic drew upwards of 6000 to 8000 people from Toronto, the Niagara region and New York State. It was a major event on the calendar of Black Torontonians for three decades.

Emancipation Day celebrations have been held in August every year in some part of Ontario since 1834. The day is now commemorated in Amherstburg, Owen Sound, Collingwood, and, since 1997, in Toronto.

provided shelter, food, clothing, money and other forms of assistance to fugitives. Today's First Baptist Church is now located on Huron Street, north of Dundas.

African Torontonians founded the Coloured Wesleyan Church in the early 1830s. At first, Blacks worshipped with whites, but withdrew because they objected to the way they were treated by the white congregations. These Black Wesleyans purchased property in 1838 on Richmond Street where they erected a building. Reverend Stephen Dutton was the first pastor of this church.

Another important focus of Black Toronto life was the African Methodist Episcopal Church (AME) that met on Sayre Street. In 1856, some AME churches broke off from

Toronto, Canada West. From the top of the Jail, 1854. E. Whitfield, artist. Courtesy of the City of Toronto Archives SC 498, Item 19.

their parent body in the United States and founded a separate denomination which was entirely Canadian in character, the British Methodist Episcopal Church (BME).

These and other churches serving the Black community were led by able and highly dedicated ministers, including the charismatic Reverend Washington Christian. In his day, he was noted for establishing more Baptist Churches than any other preacher in Canada. Another minister Reverend William M. Mitchell, had been an active Underground Railroad worker in Ohio before coming to lead the

The land for the present First Baptist Chapel, on the corner of Huron and D'Arcy streets, was purchased in 1955. From 1841 to 1905, the congregation worshipped in the First Baptist Chapel on the northeast corner of Victoria and Queen streets. Photograph by Merlin Cain. Courtesy of the First Baptist Church Archives.

The African Methodist Episcopal (AME) Church at Richmond and York streets, April 1913. Courtesy of Toronto Public Library (TPL): T33461.

Teraulay Street Baptist congregation. He travelled to Britain in the 1850s to raise money for the construction of a church, and wrote a book describing the activities of African-American immigrants in Canada. Robert M. Johnson of Indiana came to the city in 1854 as a minister for the AME church, and was an active member of the Toronto Literary Society.

The churches served as the centres of benevolent, intellectual and political life in the community. Anti-slavery speakers including the famous former slave Frederick Douglass, British abolitionist George Thompson, and Boston anti-slavery speaker Samuel J. May, all delivered addresses from the pulpits of Toronto's Baptist, AME, BME and Coloured Wesleyan Methodist churches. Charitable activities, including those for the benefit of the ever-increasing numbers of fugitive slaves arriving in the provinces, also operated from the church buildings. Activist ministers such as William P. Newman, himself an escaped slave who had been educated at Oberlin College in Ohio, spent several years working between American and Canadian congregations. He also was engaged in a series of colonization schemes to encourage Black Canadians to settle in the Caribbean. Although there was a series of such efforts, most African-American immigrants to Toronto stayed in Canada West, today's Ontario.

View of Toronto looking northwest from the corner of King and York streets, 1857.
Courtesy of City of Toronto Culture Division, Market Gallery Collection.

5 Life in the City

Toronto in the mid-1800s was a "walking" city. People lived near the places where they worked, close to the churches they attended and, if possible, near enough to a public school for their children to gain an education.

On first arrival, former slaves and free Black immigrants often boarded with families in St. John's Ward. The area lay north of Queen Street, and was bounded on the west by University Avenue and on the east by Yonge Street. Although the city did not have a defined Black neighbourhood, St. John's Ward was a favourite place of residence for many immigrant families, Black and white. Some streets such as Centre Street, which ran north from behind Osgoode Hall, as far as present day College Street, had a substantial African-American refugee population. The north end of the street was the chosen location for fugitive slaves originating in Baltimore, Maryland.

William Still, of the Philadelphia Vigilance Committee, the son of former slaves, assisted literally hundreds of slaves on their way to the Northern States and on to Canada. He recorded the stories of many who later made Toronto their home.

James Burrell, a runaway from Virginia, sent a letter to Still once he arrived, to say that he was boarding with Robert Phillips, who lived behind Osgoode Hall in 1854. Two years later, runaways James Monroe, Peter Heines, Henry James Morris and Matthew Bodams, all from North Carolina, informed Still that they were sharing rented rooms at Mr. George Blunt's, just up the street from the Phillips' home. Many other African-American immigrants lived on adjacent streets like Elizabeth, Agnes, Teraulay

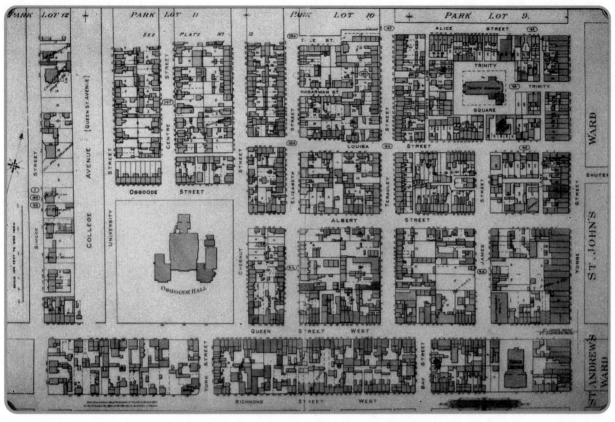

Fire insurance map of St. John's Ward where many of Toronto's recent African-American immigrants lived. From Goad's Atlas, Toronto: 1883, Plate #9.

and Albert, several of which disappeared in the redevelopment of the Eaton Centre block. Others owned businesses further west along Bathurst, Queen and Portland streets, and eastwards in the area of St. Lawrence Market and along Church Street.

New immigrants, Black and white, could afford to live in the modest one- and two-storey wooden houses lining the narrow streets of St. John's and later St. Patrick's Ward, just to the west. A dynamic Black community had grown up in the district. Education was a priority; in Toronto, public schools provided free education without regard to colour. At the end of a long working week, their parents and grandparents learned to read and write in the Sabbath Schools run by three area African-Canadian churches.

African-American immigrants possessed skills and abilities that gave them a head start in their new land. By 1850, Black Torontonians owned homes and businesses in several parts of town. Wilson Ruffin Abbott, who had arrived in 1835 and originally worked as a tobacconist, was the wealthiest member of the community. His real

The building at #94 Albert Street was occupied by Wilson Ruffin Abbott in the 1850s. Courtesy of City of Toronto Archives, Series 372, Subseries 55, Item #49.

GREAT ATTRACTION !

New Fancy Dry Goods,

AND

DRESS MAKING

ESTABLISHMENT,

York Street, between Richmond and Adelaide,

TORONTO.

MRS. M. O. AUGUSTA

RESPECTFULLY announces to the Citizens of Toronto, and vicinity, that she has just OPENED, at the stand formerly occupied by Miss STYLES, York Street, a handsome assortment of *FALL GOODS*, which she will sell as cheap as can be elsewhere obtained in the City.

The Fashions,

M. O. A. would also invite the attention of the Ladies to the

Dress Making Department,

where will at all times be found the

LATEST PARIS AND LONDON PATTERNS,

For Ladies Dresses, Mantillas, Cloaks, Sacks, and Children's Clothing.

All of which will be made to order on the shortest notice, and by the most competent hands.

☞ *An early call is respectfully solicited.*

A good MILLINER and APPRENTICES wanted September 23rd, 1854.   27

Advertisement for Mrs. Augusta's fancy dress shop. In Provincial Freeman, October 28, 1854.

estate holdings extended as far north as Owen Sound. John Tinsley and his son, Richard, were also very successful, and regularly employed newly-arrived fugitives in their carpentry business on Agnes Street, where the Eaton Centre is today. Skilled cooks owned restaurants and taverns that also provided jobs – The Tontine Coffee House was operated by Daniel Bloxom at 150 King Street East and the popular Epicurean Recess Restaurant at Church and Colborne was the property of Mr. B.R. Snow.

As more and more runaways reached Toronto, the city gained a number of blacksmiths, like Charles Peyton Lucas, carpenters and masons. A number of women became hairdressers, milliners or dressmakers. Mrs. M.O. Augusta, wife of one of the city's two Black doctors, had a successful ladies accessory store on York Street. Willis Addison was a plasterer living at Bathurst and Queen, while Matthew Truss, a shoemaker, had his own shop on Queen near Church. Mrs. Frances Teackle, a widow, was a confectioner and candy maker who lived on Centre Street, north of Osgoode Hall. Barber William Hickman's wife ran the family grocery store on York Street, while Mr. and Mrs. Phillip Judah operated a fine fruit and vegetable shop at Queen and Beverley streets.

Still other former slaves had worked in service, and thus gained a variety of skills that could be turned into gainful employment, such as barbering, operating a tobacco shop or doing fancy ironing. Some men, like Benjamin Hollinger, worked on ships that plied the Great Lakes, while others worked as waiters in the fine dining rooms of Toronto's luxury hotels. Widows sometimes operated boarding houses or rented out flats or houses to support their children. In a large city like Toronto there was always employment for those with fewer skills, labourers and dockworkers, draymen and porters, and housekeepers and washerwomen.

Bloor Street West in the 1800s.
Courtesy of the City of Toronto Archives, RG8 Series 14, Vol. 1A, Item 11.

6 Living on the Outskirts

Some African-American immigrants settled in the downtown core, while others headed to the outskirts of the city. In fact, the Township of York held the second highest population of Blacks outside of St. John's Ward in Toronto proper. In 1861, York township was a large area of land surrounding the city of Toronto, bounded by the Humber River on the west, Scarborough township on the east, and Lake Ontario and the city limits at Bloor Street on the south. Yonge Street separated York Township East from York Township West.

What attracted these immigrants to the fringes of the urban world? As was the case with many African-American migrants, these settlers were drawn to a more rural environment such as the one they had known in the United States. Some farmed while other families were attracted to the cheaper land prices, lower taxes and the greater availability of a good-sized lot for gardening, keeping a cow, a couple of pigs or some chickens. Being close to the city provided ready markets for those engaged in market gardening, as some were. Many of the men were labourers who performed such tasks as clearing land, chopping wood, hauling goods by horse and cart, building barns and houses, and doing seasonal farm work. Women also worked in the fields, as market gardeners and as washerwomen. A few women worked as servants in private households, saloons and hotels. Married women and widows also earned money by taking in boarders, usually single men.

In 1861, many families of note lived In Ward 3 of York Township West, where

Pioneer Hotel in Seaton Village at the corner of Bathurst and Bloor streets, circa 1890. This building was a couple of blocks from the house of Deborah Brown. Courtesy of Toronto Public Library (TPL): T 11049.

Deborah Brown made her home. In this particular district lived the highest number of African Canadians and African-American immigrants found in all of York township. Well-known Underground Railroad refugees, the Wanzers and Grigsbys, were two families living close by. They shared a one-storey frame house on the lot next to Deborah and Perry Brown. Frank and Emily Wanzer were 30 and 28 years of age respectively and Barnaby and Mary Grigsby were 33 and 30 respectively, according to the census taker. The Wanzers owned a horse and four pigs, all valued at $15, and the couples lived on one-half acre of land. The two men were labourers and both couples worshipped in the Wesleyan Methodist faith.

The Wanzers had two additions to their family by 1861. Two-year-old Mary Wanzer and one-year-old George had both been born in Canada. The Grigsby family did not have any children.

Another neighbour of Deborah Brown was the Reverend W.M. Mitchell, his wife

Jefferson and Mary Pipkins

One of the heart-wrenching aspects of escape on the Underground Railroad, as has been seen, was the fact that children often had to be left behind. Jefferson and Mary L. Pipkins (or Pipkin) who were also neighbours of Deborah Brown and her husband, escaped from Baltimore, Maryland, in April 1853, and found their way to the Philadelphia Vigilance Committee. With the help of the anti-slavery network in Philadelphia and New York, the Pipkins ultimately settled in York Township West, near the Browns, the Wanzers and the Grigsbys. Several years after their escape, as the following letter from Jefferson Pipkins illustrates, the couple was still trying to find a way out of slavery for their four children:

Sept. 28, 1856.

> To Wm. Still. Sir:
> I take the liberty of writing to you a few lines concerning my children, for I am anxious to get them and I wish you to please try what you can do for me. Their names are Charles and Patrick and are living with Mrs. Joseph G. Wray Murphysborough Hartford county, North Carolina; Emma lives with a lawyer Baker in Gatesville North Carolina and Susan lives in Portsmouth Virginia and is stopping with Dr. Collins sister a Mrs. Nash ... And I trust you will try what you think will be the best way. And you will do me a great favor. Yours Respectfully,
>
> Jefferson Pipkins.
>
> P.S. I am living at Yorkville near Toronto Canada West. My wife sends her best respects to Mrs. Still.

William Still, of the Philadelphia Vigilance Committee, noted that, sadly, nothing could be done by the Committee to abduct relatives still in slavery because it was simply too dangerous. By 1861, it is known that Mr. and Mrs. Pipkins were still living in York Township West and that none of their children were living with them in the household. Jefferson Pipkins, aged 60, was employed as a labourer and his wife Mary was reported to be 48 years of age and, as was usually the case for wives, had no employment listed beside her name in the census.

Did the couple ever see their children again? Incredibly, one child may have joined her mother after Emancipation. By 1871, Jefferson Pipkins was dead. An Emma Pipkins was listed as living with Mary Pipkins in the 1871 and 1881 censuses for York township. Could this be the Emma mentioned as living in slavery in North Carolina? The Emma named in the 1871 census was reported as born in Ontario and aged 10 years old. She was also reported to be "English" as compared with Mary Pipkins' designation as "African." She appeared again with Mary Pipkins in the 1881 census, and this time neither are listed as "African." These discrepancies probably reflect the ignorance of the census taker, who may have mistaken light skin for whiteness. Interestingly, in contrast to the 1871 census, in which no occupation was given, Emma was described as a dressmaker. Mary Pipkins was described as a laundress.

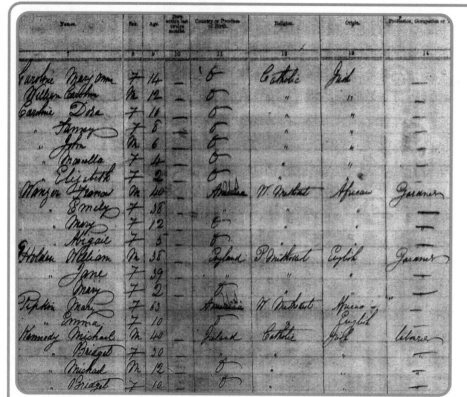

In 1871, Mary Pipkins was 63 years of age. She was perhaps too old to be the child's mother. Could Emma have been her grandchild? It is also entirely possible that Mary Pipkins reunited with one or more of her children and that she was raising one of her grandchildren. Her children may simply have been living in a separate household elsewhere. Although we may never be able to solve this mystery, it would certainly be nice to speculate that Mary Pipkins reunited with at least one of her children.

Elizabeth and their five children. Reverend Mitchell was a Baptist minister and abolitionist who was active in the African-Canadian community of Toronto. The Mitchell family lived in a one-storey frame house on a three-quarters-acre plot of land. At the time, the Reverend was in England speaking on behalf of the African community in Canada and raising funds for his church. He preached at the Coloured Regular Baptist Church in St. John's Ward, downtown Toronto.

Reverend Mitchell may have obtained a ride to the church each Sunday with the Richards family in their horse-drawn buggy or wagon. Richard B. Richards was a respected member and trustee of the Coloured Regular Baptist Church, and he and his family would have attended the downtown church on a regular basis.

In addition to his stature among Black Baptists, Richard B. Richards owned a successful ice business and lived on a three acre farm on Davenport Road in Ward 3. In addition to his own wife and three grown children, Richards' brothers and brother-in-law and their families lived on the property. Richards' daughters Harriet, aged 26, and Nancy, aged 25, worked as a tailoress and dressmaker, respectively. His son William, aged 22, was a grocer by trade. G.W. Carter, most likely Richards' son-in-law, was a barber living with his wife and four-year-old daughter. Henry Richards, another brother, a labourer, was a widower with four children aged 11 to 21.

These families represent the different levels of social and economic status that Black people had attained in the province. Often, the length of time a family had been in Canada determined how well they were succeeding in their new environment and how much property they had been able to acquire. This was true of all new immigrants to the province.

Although escape was both difficult and dangerous, some fugitive men and women were able to bring their children. From Harriet Beecher Stowe, *Uncle Tom's Cabin; or, Life Among the Lowly* (Toronto: Thomas Maclear, 1852). Toronto Public Library, Special Collections, Genealogy & Maps Centre.

7 The World of Children

Whenever possible, fugitive slaves moving to Toronto brought their children with them. Many examples exist of men and women who, once free, desperately tried to purchase or even steal their children away from Southern slaveholders. Free people, too, who had formerly lived in the Northern United States came to Toronto in family groups throughout the period before the Civil War.

One interesting example was Elizabeth Hudson, her husband William, and their children. Their path from slavery to freedom can be traced through the birthplaces of their five children. Their eldest son, Thomas Henry Hudson was born in North Carolina, while his parents were still enslaved. By the time Clara Elizabeth arrived, the family had escaped to Connecticut, moving in the next year even further away from Southern slave catchers by settling in Boston, where William was born. By 1861, they are recorded as living on Toronto's Centre Street, behind Osgoode Hall, and had a daughter Selia, born after their arrival.

Life in early Toronto was difficult for infants and children. Various epidemics swept through the downtown core in the nineteenth century. Cholera is said to have killed one in four Torontonians in 1857. Disease was most deadly in areas of high population concentration, and where outdoor toilets existed side-by-side with public wells. These were common conditions in early Toronto, and children of the rich and poor alike were victims of deadly illness.

Immunization was not yet common and medical care was still primitive. Cemetery

Toronto Shoeshine Boy, *1898, Joshua Beihn, artist. Artworks of African Canadians in Toronto are extremely rare. While the detail here is striking, the work portrays a negatively stereotypic image of a shoeshine boy in Toronto at the turn of the twentieth century.* Courtesy of City of Toronto Culture Division, Market Gallery Art Collection.

records show that many babies died of what today would be minor illnesses; infections and fever were responsible for many infant deaths, as were childhood illnesses like measles, chickenpox and mumps.

It was particularly poignant to note that the Wanzer family, who had overcome so much just to reach Canada, lost four youngsters in the space of 12 years. Three died as infants, including little George F. Wanzer, who was only a one-year-old during the time of the 1861 census and who died half a year later of consumption (tuberculosis). Another infant, Frank, died in 1869 at four months old of whooping cough, and a third, Nathaniel, at three months, 11 days, of teething in 1870. This last cause of death may seem particularly shocking, but it was not uncommon in the nineteenth century. The child could have died of a fever associated with teething or his gums might have been lanced to allow the teeth to come through, causing him to die of infection. Most tragic of all, however, may have been the death of Mary E. Wanzer at the age of 14. She died of an abscess in 1873.

High infant mortality rates were a fact of life. Indeed, many families lived with one or more tragedies of this nature. Reverend Mitchell's daughter Eliza, who had been born in Ohio, died of inflammation in 1861 at the age of six years, eleven months. These untimely deaths also suggest the lack of adequate health care and the absence of qualified medical personnel on the fringes of the urban environment. By this time, many of these children, as well as their parents, were buried in the Toronto

Schoolroom in the Victoria Industrial School (Toronto) in 1898.
Courtesy of Toronto Public Library (TPL): T 14120.

Necropolis Cemetery, on Winchester Farm across from today's Riverdale Farm.

Like all immigrant groups in the nineteenth century city, many African-Canadian families were forced to send their children to work. Very little record exists of the lives of working Black children but most likely they sold newspapers, worked as whitewashers, shined shoes and laboured in the foundries, blacksmith shops, tanneries and livery stables in early Toronto.

However, a very strong emphasis on education characterized the African-Canadian society. In most American states before the Civil War, it was against the law to teach a slave to read. This was because slaveholders were afraid that their human "property" would acquire ideas about freedom from what they read, especially if they were reading the Bible or any of the many booklets and articles published by American anti-slavery groups. Once they reached Canada, however, former slaves wanted nothing more than to acquire an education for their children, and also for themselves. Churches operated "Sabbath Schools" and night schools, teaching adults to read alongside their children.

Pupils of Ogden Public School, Toronto, circa 1900. Courtesy of the Museum and Archives, Toronto District School Board.

Toronto was unique in nineteenth-century Canada in that the public schools and schools of higher learning were always open to Black students. In most parts of the province, Black immigrants to Canada were forced to found and support private schools, because local school officials barred children of colour. Parents sent petition after petition to government officials, demanding that schooling be made available, often with little result.

The children of the largely Black areas in St. John's and St. Patrick's wards had a choice of several schools. Census documents from 1841 and 1861 (the Toronto census for 1851 was unfortunately destroyed) list the number of children in each household who were attending school. The Toronto Board of Education operated public schools in the downtown core beginning in the middle of the nineteenth century. Louisa Street School, Phoebe Street School and Richmond Street School were all within a short walk of many African-Canadian homes. Eight-year-old William Brown, a member of Deborah Brown's household, was away attending school in the city. He was most likely boarding with relatives or another family who lived closer to one of the city schools.

Black students entered various schools of higher learning in Toronto as well. Anderson Ruffin Abbott, son of free African-American settlers Wilson Ruffin Abbott, and his wife Ellen Toyer Abbott, was the first African Canadian to graduate from King's College Medical School. Emmaline Shadd won first prize for proficiency in her year at the Toronto Normal School, as the city's teachers' college was called at the time. Also a graduate of the Normal School was James Rapier, who later went on to be the first Black Congressman from Alabama during the post-Civil War years.

Samuel Ringgold Ward was a well-known and eloquent Congregational minister. He came to Canada after participating in a famous fugitive slave rescue in Syracuse and served as agent for the Anti-Slavery Society, touring the province and giving speeches on anti-slavery. Ward was an agent of the Voice of the Fugitive *and also edited the* Provincial Freeman *with Mary Ann Shadd.* From Samuel Ringgold Ward, *Autobiography of a Fugitive Negro: His Anti-Slavery Labors in the United States, Canada, and England* (London, U.K.: John Snow, 1855) Frontispiece. Toronto Public Library, Special Collections, Genealogy & Maps Centre.

8 Political Life

Though Blacks found a measure of protection and security in Toronto, they faced discrimination and racism in many aspects of their lives. However, they did not simply let this go by. Black Torontonians' response to the minstrel shows illustrates how they fought negative stereotypes and racism.

In the nineteenth century, "Black" minstrel shows were a common feature of entertainment. The actors, in fact, were neither Black nor of African heritage, but white people who smeared their faces and bodies with soot or shoe polish. Then, on stage, they would mimic what they believed to be "Black" behaviour. White audiences enjoyed these performances; Blacks did not. African Canadians all over the province felt that minstrel shows insulted and demeaned Black people, their way of life and their culture.

As in other major cities across North America, in Toronto such minstrel shows were frequently performed. In 1840, African Torontonians took a stand against them. Led by Wilson Ruffin Abbott, 45 members of the Black community signed a petition and went to City Hall. They asked the mayor and the Council to prohibit the performance of minstrel shows in the city. A vote was taken in council, but unfortunately, the majority did not support Abbott and his colleagues. This did not deter them, for two years later they tried again. This time they won, and so the minstrel shows that for so long had disparaged Black people were not perfomed in Toronto for some years, but would later be revived.

One reason for their success was that in the City of Toronto, the Black vote was important. And politicians of either of the two major parties desired that the Black voters support them in elections. They knew that often, Black voters could determine the outcome of elections.

Anti-slavery or abolitionism activities were central to the political life of Black Toronto. Beginning in the 1830s and continuing for another 30 years, Toronto was a hub of anti-slavery sentiment. Slavery in the United States was not abolished until after the Civil War, and Black Torontonians kept up a constant agitation against American slavery. Every day, fugitive slaves arrived on the Underground Railroad.

VOICE OF THE FUGITIVE.

HENRY BIBB, EDITOR.   SANDWICH, C. W., MARCH 12, 1851.   VOL. I, NO. 6.

Many free Blacks also made the trip and settled in Toronto. Many of the Black anti-slavery leaders in the city were themselves fugitive slaves and so they had a first-hand knowledge of the horrors of American slavery.

St. Lawrence Hall on King Street East was a cultural, social and political centre of the city. It was here in February 1851, that an interracial group, including two Scots, George Brown, publisher of the *Globe*, and Michael Willis, Principal of Knox College, as well as Black abolitionists, publisher Henry Bibb and A.B. Jones, of London, Canada West, founded the Anti-Slavery Society of Canada. Soon after its beginning, the Society invited renowned abolitionists, the British George Thompson, the American Samuel Joseph May, and the eloquent former slave Frederick Douglass himself, to lecture at the Hall. They spoke to packed audiences and did much to encourage many people to join the cause.

Perhaps the most important event to occur in Toronto also took place in 1851. The North American Convention of Coloured People was called and chaired by Henry Walton Bibb, himself a fugitive slave. He had only been in Canada for about a year. Following the publication of his successful autobiography, Bibb and his wife Mary Miles Bibb, a schoolteacher and fellow abolitionist, had moved from the United States. Once across the border, he established Canada's first Black newspaper, the *Voice of the Fugitive*, published in Sandwich, near Windsor. This paper championed the cause of Canadian Blacks and called for their full civil rights. The Convention met at St. Lawrence Hall. For three days, more than 53 delegates discussed the safety and security of Black people in North America, and ways to improve Black life on the continent. Finally, on the third and

Kentucky-born Henry Bibb escaped from slavery in 1842. Arriving in Detroit he joined the abolitionist movement and became one of the most renowned anti-slavery activists and lecturers of his day. This formal photograph of Henry Walton Bibb, taken in 1849 when he was 34 years of age, became the frontispiece for his published autobiography, Narrative of the Life and Adventures of Henry Bibb, An American Slave, *published that year. The book became an instant best-seller and went through three printings in 18 months. From* Narrative of the Life and Adventures of Henry Bibb: An American Slave *(1849). Toronto Public Library, Special Collections, Genealogy & Maps Centre.*

St. Lawrence Hall as it looks today. Courtesy of the Archaeological Resource Centre, Toronto District School Board.

final day, Henry Bibb, James Tinsley and John Fisher, gave an address, which summed up the sentiments of the delegates on the questions at hand. The delegates concluded that Canada – with Jamaica running second – was the best place for Blacks on the North American continent. Bibb urged American slaves to run away, and appealed to free Blacks to come settle in Canada, and take up farming in order to be self-sufficient. In addition, the delegates also praised Canada for giving refuge to Black people:

> Resolved, that we feel truly grateful, as a people, to her Britannic Majesty's just and powerful government, for the protection afforded us; and are fully persuaded from the known fertility of the soil, and salubrity of climate of the milder regions of Canada West, that this is, by far, the most desirable place of resort for colored people, to be found on the American continent.

The John Anderson Trial

John Anderson in Montreal, 1861. Courtesy of McCord Museum, Notman Photographic Archives 1-0555.

The John Anderson Extradition trial was an event that galvanized the Black and abolitionist communities in Toronto. Anderson was a Missouri-born slave who, in 1851, decided to flee from slavery. A white slaveholder Seneca Diggs, tried to prevent Anderson's flight. A tussle ensued in which Anderson pulled a knife and stabbed the slaveholder. He later died. However, Anderson made his way to Canada and, aided by abolitionists, he found work. Anderson moved to Brantford, Ontario, where he worked as a mason. He even bought a house. In 1859, he confided to a "friend" the story of his escape. This "friend" promptly told the authorities and in no time, Anderson was apprehended and arrested by the police.

Treaties between the British government and the United States required Canada to return proven criminals, to stand trial in American courts. The government of the United States, on hearing that Anderson was arrested, called for his immediate return to face the court.

The Court of the Queen's Bench in Toronto, presided over by Chief Justice John Beverly Robinson, ruled, on November 15, 1861, that Anderson must be returned to the United States to face trial. There was a huge outcry at Robinson's ruling. Everyone knew that, if returned, Anderson would face certain death. Missouri was known for its "lynch law." That meant that Blacks could and did not have fair trials under Missouri laws because it was a slave state in which Blacks had little or no rights.

The media, especially the Toronto Globe, castigated Robinson for his decision. The Globe retorted that Canada was known as a refuge for slaves and if Anderson were to be returned, American slave catchers could easily come into Canada and claim their alleged slaves. The city was in an uproar over Robinson's decision. Blacks met in the churches and denounced the ruling, vowing to ensure that Anderson would not be returned to Missouri. The abolitionist community held meetings at City Hall and at the St. Lawrence Hall.

The trial of John Anderson was held in Osgoode Hall in 1861. The building is still standing on the corner of Queen Street and University Avenue. Courtesy of the Archives of Ontario S1175.

One American abolitionist, Gerrit Smith came from Syracuse and spoke at the St. Lawrence Hall. Smith urged the Black and abolitionist communities to prevent the extradition of Anderson.

Anderson's lawyer and members of the Black and abolitionist communities appealed to the Privy Council in England, the highest court in the British Empire, and therefore the highest court of appeal for Canadians at that time. The Privy Council ruled in favour of Anderson, noting that slavery was wrong and against "natural rights" and that Anderson was justified in defending himself against a man who wanted to enslave him.

However, a local Toronto court, the Court of Common Pleas, presided over by Judge Henry Draper, also ruled in favour of Anderson. Draper stated that Anderson should not be extradited. There was great rejoicing in the city at Draper's decision. Marches, dinners and meetings were held by Black Torontonians celebrating Anderson's victory. Anderson himself gave speeches and thanked his Black and white supporters. A few months later, still fearing for his safety (he thought the Americans would still try to extradite him) Anderson travelled to England where he attended college. He later migrated to Liberia, West Africa.

Toronto's Black women and men drew on their own resources to build a viable political life in the city. African Canadians sometimes made alliances with sympathetic whites in their struggle for a life of dignity. The Anti-Slavery Society of Canada is a sterling example of Black and white co-operation in the fight against racism, slavery and discrimination.

The various reform organizations, such as the Provincial Union, the Queen Victoria Benevolent Society and the Ladies Fugitive Society, should not only be seen as philanthropic groups, but, given the nature of their activism, also as political organizations. Years later, the son of a fugitive slave would rise to the top of Toronto's political arena. William Hubbard, a baker by trade, was elected to the City Council in 1894 and served as Deputy Mayor of the city from 1904 to 1907.

Anderson Ruffin Abbott in Civil War uniform. Courtesy of Toronto Public Library (TPL): Manuscript Collection (S90) Abbott Papers.

9 Black Torontonians in the Civil War

Many African Canadians fought in the Union Army during the American Civil War. This war was set into motion over the issue of "state's rights" or the right of each territory or state to choose between being a slave state or a free state. When the slave states of the American South began to separate from the Union over this issue, the Civil War broke out in April 1861.

Toronto has always had close ties to the United States. As an important port on the Great Lakes, the commercial enterprises of the city regularly did business with American cities like Buffalo and Rochester. Railways linked Toronto with Chicago and Detroit, and with Upper New York State. Companies that did business in both countries maintained offices in both Toronto and cities in the United States. Canadian newspapers like the *Globe* regularly reported on American events. Toronto, too, was a hotbed of anti-slavery activism, involving both Black and white, for decades before the Civil War. Abolitionists in Canada worked with American anti-slavery forces to bring an end to Southern slavery.

American-born Black people who migrated to Toronto remained committed to ending slavery in the United States, as well as to helping make conditions better for Black Americans living in the North. They maintained ties with family, friends and associates south of the border. Many who fled Southern slavery left behind parents, children and dearly loved husbands or wives. Free African Americans who had moved from cities like Philadelphia, New York and Cincinnati in search of better opportunities for their families stayed in touch with relatives and business partners in the United States.

Foremost in everyone's mind in the middle of the 1800s was the threat of war in the United States. The North and South could not agree whether slavery should be allowed in the newly forming states of the western frontier. As the conflict continued, and after war was formally declared, it became apparent that if the Union Army of the North defeated the Confederate Army of the South, slavery would end in the United States.

Black Canadians made a very significant contribution to the war effort, and so helped set free the more than four million Americans enslaved in the Southern states. Many families living in Toronto sent their sons to fight and die so that the institution of slavery would forever be destroyed in North America.

On January 1, 1863, President Abraham Lincoln issued the Emancipation Proclamation, which promised freedom for slaves in all the states of the Confederacy, but did not include states such as Kentucky that were part of the Union, even though Kentucky had slavery. Toronto's African-Canadian churches held services for men going to fight on the Union side in the Civil War. After two years of bloody fighting, President Lincoln had finally decided to enlist the thousands of African Americans who volunteered for the Union Army. African Canadians also flocked to enlist in Michigan's 102nd Colored Troops, the 5th Massachusetts (Colored) Cavalry and the 55th Massachusetts (Colored) Infantry. Mary Ann Shadd Cary, an important abolitionist and newspaper publisher who once lived in Toronto, moved from Chatham, Canada West, to Detroit to become the Union Army's only female recruiting officer.

Canadian Black men who went to fight ranged from sailors and waiters through physicians and teachers. Not all came home. Abraham Brown died in South Carolina in 1863, only six months after he joined up, and Privates William Jackson and John E. Annick, of Toronto, both survived the hostilities and were discharged at the end of the war in August of 1865.

Medical men from Toronto rose high in the ranks of Black Union Army officers. Dr. A.T. Augusta, of Virginia, had trained at Toronto's Trinity College before becoming the official physician for the city's Poor House. A distinguished surgeon, he was the first Major commissioned in the Union Army. After the war he stayed in Washington DC. Anderson Ruffin Abbott, the first Canadian-born Black doctor to graduate from Kings College Medical School, studied under Augusta in Toronto. Also a distinguished surgeon in the Union Army, he became Assistant Director of the Freedmen's Bureau Hospital in Washington, DC. He was entertained at the White House and later received, from Mrs. Lincoln, a shawl once worn by the President, as a token of esteem.

When President Lincoln was shot in Ford's Theatre in April of 1865, Toronto was plunged into mourning. Both Black and white churches held memorial services, and historian Dr. Daniel Hill tells us that a mass meeting of Black Torontonians was held to commemorate the life and good deeds of the Great Emancipator (as Lincoln was called).

In August of 1865, the Civil War ended. The forces that fought to keep the North and South together as one united country had prevailed. The threat of separation of the southern states was over. There was much celebration in the African-American and African-Canadian communities.

With the end of the Civil War and the emancipation of the American slaves, the engines of the Underground Railroad grew silent. Black Americans were finally free to make their own way — to live off the sweat of their own brow. Some African Canadians felt the need to make a "return trip" south to find and reunite with families and loved ones from whom they had been separated. Many of the well-educated became teachers, doctors, lawyers and politicians during the Reconstruction Era, which was intended to rebuild society after the war and help former slaves make their way in freedom. Many historians believe that most African Canadians returned to the United States following the Civil War. New research, however, shows that

Dr. A.T. (Alexander Thomas) Augusta in his Civil War uniform.
Courtesy of the Dan Hill Collection, National Archives of Canada PA 211254.

Tintype of an uniden-
tified Black soldier of
the Union Army, Civil
War (1861-1865).
Courtesy of the Chicago
Historical Society ICHi-
08060.

many people remained in Canada and brought newly freed relatives back to live with them in their new country.

Unfortunately, the tide of history shifted again as Europe colonized Africa beginning in the 1880s and with the rise of Jim Crow laws[1] in the United States that barred African Americans from the fruits of full citizenship. Reconstruction was swept away and in its wake, a new racist society emerged. Black people in Canada did not have racist laws enacted against them, but nevertheless they were greatly affected by this climate of anti-Black feeling. Canada's role as a haven for escaped slaves was no more and whites were no longer as accepting of Blacks as they had been. Caricatures of Black people appeared routinely in the press and mass media. In 1850, no fewer than sixteen Black businesses were thriving on King Street. By the turn of the century, Black businesses were few and far between. African Canadians were kept at the bottom of the social class system, often in the lowest paying and most servile occupations. It was a cruel twist of fate for those who had risked everything to live under "the Lion's paw of British freedom," as it was termed. But African Canadians forged on, knowing that a better day would dawn.

Black soldiers in the Civil War, Company "E," 4th U.S. Infantry, Fort Lincoln, Virginia. Published by Taylor & Huntington, photographer unknown. Courtesy of Chicago Historical Society, ICHi 07784.

Left: Thomas Powers Casey owned a successful barber- and hairdressing shop in St. Catharines until relocating to the Rossin House Hotel, Toronto, in 1867. Here, Thomas Powers Casey is shown with two of his three daughters. From l to r: Henrietta Margaret (married Phillip Judah), Hannah Elizabeth (married Levi Lightfoot) and Thomas, their father. Courtesy of the Daniel Hill Collection, National Archives of Canada PA 211257.

Below: Daughter Mary Ann Casey became the wife of Anderson R. Abbott, photo circa 1875. Courtesy of the Daniel Hill Collection, National Archives of Canada PA 211255.

10 Notable Black Torontonians

The Black fugitives and freepersons who made Toronto their home during the Underground Railroad era contributed to the growth and development of the city. Our research unveiled the biographies – some extensive, some meagre – of many of these people. All of the personages encountered, whether they led public or obscure lives, left a mark on history. It was decided to create a gallery of "notable" people who contributed in one way or another to the development of Toronto's Black community and to the city as a whole. The number of significant people made selection difficult. Consequently, the decision was made to highlight not just the "famous" ones like the brilliant medical doctor Alexander T. Augusta but also the "ordinary" folk exemplified by the indomitable fugitive slave washerwoman Ann Maria Jackson. The biographies that follow, therefore, represent a broad cross-section of the people who developed a vibrant Black culture and participated in the growth and maturation of the city.

The Abbott Family

Wilson Ruffin Abbott, born of a free woman in Richmond, Virginia, would later become the wealthiest African-Canadian resident of Toronto, Upper Canada. He arrived in his new home in 1835 with his wife, Ellen Toyer Abbott, a free Black woman from Baltimore who had already taught her husband to read and write. They had left behind in Mobile, Alabama, a prosperous grocery business, but, finding life in the American South too repressive and dangerous for free Black families, they moved first to New York and then to Canada.

Abbott was a lifelong opponent of slavery and racial oppression, serving on numerous committees and as part of various organizations throughout his long life. He helped establish self-help and benevolent groups, as well as being a founder of the Anti-Slavery Society of Canada and also of the Coloured Wesleyan Methodist Church. His wife was President of the Queen Victoria Benevolent Society, a Black women's charitable organization. In his later life, Abbott was elected to the Toronto City Council. When Wilson Ruffin Abbott passed away in 1876, he left a substantial estate including more than 40 houses stretching from Owen Sound on Georgian Bay to Toronto and Hamilton.

Phillip Judah and his wife Henrietta (Casey) on the porch of the home of William P. Hubbard, 660 Broadview, following the death of his wife in 1915. Courtesy of the Daniel Hill Collection, National Archives of Canada PA 211251.

The Abbotts' four sons and five daughters were educated and accomplished individuals, and their second son, Anderson, was the first Canadian-born Black doctor to graduate from Toronto's King's College Medical School. He became one of only eight Black surgeons in the Union Army, and was Assistant Director of the Freedmen's Bureau Hospital in Washington DC during Reconstruction, after the war ended.

ADOLPHUS AND PHILLIP JUDAH

The Judahs were another important African American immigrant family to make their mark on Toronto life. Adolphus married Ellen Toyer Abbott's sister, Jane and rapidly rose to prominence through his dedication to the causes of education and self-sufficiency for the African-Canadian community. He vigorously encouraged Black Torontonians to participate in the political life of the city. Judah was a staunch supporter of anti-slavery activities in Toronto, and was central to the establishment of the Coloured Regular Baptist congregation on Teraulay Street. He was a founder of the Provincial Union Association, the organizational arm of the *Provincial Freeman* newspaper and the Association for the Education and Elevation of Coloured People.

Adolphus H. Judah later moved to Chatham, Canada West, where he supported the Elgin Association and the fugitive slave colony founded by Reverend William King at Buxton. His son, Phillip, continued to play an important role in Black Toronto's political and community life. He operated a fancy green grocery store at the northwest corner of Queen Street at Beverley. The building is still standing today, an HMV music store.

THE HICKMAN FAMILY

The Hickmans came to Toronto in the 1830s from Virginia. William Hickman Sr., a barber, had been freed because he fought in both the American Revolution and in the War of 1812 on the American side. But former slaves could not stay in Virginia after they received their freedom, so he moved to Toronto with his son and daughter in about 1833. Hickman took part in the city's early anti-slavery activities. Together with J.C. Brown and Stephen Dutton, two of the founders of the Wilberforce Settlement located north of London, he owned land in the Oro area north of Barrie, where a number of American Black families had settled.

William Hickman's son and grandson, both named William, were business people in Toronto by the 1850s. They owned land on York Street, just south of Osgoode

A directory listing for Hickman, W. and Hickman, Wm. Jr. From Rowsell's City of Toronto and County of York's Dirctory, (Toronto, 1850-51) 60.

Hall, and operated a barber shop and grocery stores in the area. Nearby were a number of other Black-owned businesses. James Mink's hotel and livery stable were just around the corner, and across the street was the fancy ladies' accessory shop of Mrs. M.O. Augusta. Next door to the Hickman home was a house owned by Peter Gallego, a very promising Black student at the university. The Hickman family had a practical approach to helping fugitive slaves; they built extra housing in the backyards of their downtown properties so that newcomers would have somewhere to live when they first came to Toronto.

James Mink

Mr. Mink was a familiar sight on Toronto's downtown streets, for he operated the city's largest livery stable as well as a fancy hotel, the Mansion House, near the corner of Richmond and York streets. He was the son of an enslaved couple brought to Canada from Pennsylvania with the celebrated United Empire Loyalist family, the Herkimers. James' brother George, operated a stage coach business in Kingston and, between the two of them, the Minks dominated postal transport between Kingston and Toronto, as well as the transfer of prisoners to and from the penitentiary set in their city.

James Mink often billed the mayor and city council for the use of his carriages and horses. In his later life, James Mink lost much of his fortune. Mink had married off his beloved daughter to a white cab man from Yorkshire, who took her to the United States on a honeymoon and there sold his bride into slavery. It was some years before Mink could gain his daughter's freedom. Discouraged, he retired to his home in Richmond Hill, where he spent the later years of his life.

Thornton and Lucie Blackburn

The Blackburns' remarkable story came to light as the result of a 1985 archaeological excavation. This couple arrived in the same year that Toronto first became a city – 1834. Fugitive slaves from Kentucky, Thornton and Lucie Blackburn had escaped their Louisville owners and first made their way to Detroit, where they were recaptured two years later. The Blackburns were rescued in a highly dramatic series of events, and spirited away to Canadian shores, where they were freed.

Upon their first arrival in Toronto, the Blackburns built a small frame house on what is now Eastern Avenue at the corner of Sackville Street. Thornton's first job was as a waiter at the lawyers' dining room at Osgoode Hall. Soon, though, he and his wife went into business for themselves.

Thornton and Lucie Blackburn began the first taxi business in Upper Canada, and became prominent and prosperous members of Toronto's Black community. The Blackburn cab, painted red and yellow and drawn by a single horse, became a familiar sight on Toronto's busy streets. The Blackburns participated in anti-slavery and community-building activities, and generously donated both time and money to helping other fugitive slaves settle in their adopted home.

In 1999, the Canadian government designated the Blackburns "Persons of National Historic Significance" for their important contribution to the growth of Toronto and, in 2002, plaques in their honour were erected in Louisville, Kentucky, and Toronto, Canada, in the first commemoration of an Underground Railroad journey ever carried out between the United States and Canada.

Toronto Telegram *article about Thornton and Lucie Blackburn.* In John Ross Robertson, *Landmarks of Toronto,* Volume 2, 1896, 677-78.

THE FIRST CAB IN THE CITY.

The Early History of Public Conveyances and Some of the Men Who Drove Them.

East of Parliament street is a section of the city abounding in short, narrow streets, thickly built up with houses of moderate size. Eastern avenue is one of the thoroughfares traversing this district. No. 54 of this street is a very small one storey frame building, painted almost black by wind and weather. Here for more than fifty years has lived a well known coloured man named Thornton Blackburn. In one of the doors in his house he points out to the visitor a panel shattered by a bullet during the Mackenzie rebellion. Mr. Blackburn came from the United States to Toronto, accompanied by his wife, who is still living, in 1884. For several years he found employment as a table waiter at Osgoode Hall. Previous to this cabs had made their first appearance in Montreal copied from a vehicle then popular in London. Mr. Blackburn obtained the pattern of a Montreal cab and taking it to Paul Bishop, a French Canadian, whose name of L'Eveque —the Bishop— had been Anglicized in Upper Canada, he ordered one made from the design furnished. Bishop, who was a mechanic of great skill, and counted as the best lock-maker in Canada, had a shop at the north-east corner of Sherbourne and Duke streets. He accepted Mr. Blackburn's commission, and in 1837 he delivered to him the first cab built in Upper Canada. This cab has been on exhibition at the York Pioneer's log house in the Exhibition grounds. It was named "The City." The cab was painted yellow and red. The entrance for passengers was from the rear. There was accommodation in it for four passengers. The driver sat on his box in front. One horse drew the vehicle. For several years Mr. Blackburn had the monopoly of the cab business in Toronto.

REVEREND W.M. MITCHELL

A steel engraving of Reverend William Mitchell of Toronto. From Reverend W.M. Mitchell, *The Underground Rail Road* (London, U.K.: William Tweedie, 1860) Frontispiece.

Most Canadians of African descent did not leave a record of their thoughts and feelings about life at that time. One of the exceptions was Reverend William Mitchell, a Baptist minister and abolitionist who is perhaps best known for writing the book, *The Underground Rail Road*.

Mitchell was born free in Guildford County, North Carolina, to an Indian mother and African-American father. His parents died when he was quite young and he was raised by local authorities. Mitchell was apprenticed to a planter for twelve years and managed a plantation the last five years of his indenture. He witnessed all the cruelties and abuses of the slave system.

As a result of his experiences, after his period of indenture was up, he studied Christianity and devoted himself to the cause of the enslaved. In 1843, Mitchell moved to Ross County, Ohio, with his wife and assisted runaway slaves on the Underground Railroad. Among those he helped was the famous Eliza Harris, immortalized in Harriet Beecher Stowe's novel, *Uncle Tom's Cabin*. She escaped across the Ohio River by jumping from ice flow to ice flow, her child in her arms, so that her infant son – who had already been sold – could not be delivered to his new owner.

In 1855, Mitchell became a missionary for the American Baptist Free Mission Society and moved to Ward 3, York Township West. He pastored at the Coloured Regular Baptist Church on Terauley and Edward streets in downtown Toronto and became involved in the elevation of the Black community in Canada. For example, with Adolphus Judah, he was a member of the "Association for the Education and Elevation of the Coloured People of Canada," a race-uplift organization focused on African-Canadian youth. Reverend Mitchell lived with his wife Eliza and five children – James, John, Fred J., Eliza E. and Augusta L. – who ranged in age from two to 16 years old. They were neighbours of Deborah and Perry Brown. Between 1859 and 1861, Mitchell was in London, England, on a fundraising tour for his church. It was there that he published his anti-slavery narrative.

REVEREND WASHINGTON CHRISTIAN

Reverend Washington Christian organized one of the first Baptist congregations in Toronto. Aptly named The First Baptist Church, the pioneering congregation began meeting in 1826 on the shore of Lake Ontario. Washington soon shepherded his congregation from its outdoor meeting place to its first church building at the corners of Queen and Victoria streets. First Baptist soon emerged as a centre of Black activism in the city.

In 1842, with the church firmly established, Christian wen on a fundraising tour in the West Indies. Universally known and loved as "Elder Washington," Christian became known as a "church founder." In his day he was noted for establishing more Baptist churches than any other preacher in Canada, including those churches in Toronto, Hamilton, Niagara and St. Catharines.

RICHARD B. RICHARDS

Richard B. Richards was a successful merchant who established the first ice business in Toronto in partnership with Thomas F. Cary, a Toronto businessman and activist who married Mary Ann Shadd. The Richards were from the United States and most probably came to Canada in the 1830s. In 1854, they owned four icehouses and by 1861, Richards and his wife Sarah owned a farm with their adult children and other family members in York Township, Ward 3, on Davenport Road. Their ice business, valued in 1861 at $1,100, was at the same location on Davenport. It stored and sold 100 tons of ice for a total value of $600 annually and employed three male "hands" at an average cost per month of $8. These employees chopped huge frozen blocks from Ashbridges Bay during the winter and kept the ice insulated with sawdust during the

ICE! ICE!! ICE!!

THE Undersigned begs to return his best thanks to his Customers for the liberal patronage he has received for the last nine years, and to announce that he has enlarged and added to the number of his Ice Houses, having now four, which are filled with pure and wholesome Springwater Ice, from Yorkville. He is prepared to supply the same to consumers, by contract or otherwise, during the season, commencing from the 1st of June. In consequence of the increased cost of labor and materials, the price will this year be raised in the same proportion. The Ice will be conveyed by waggon, daily, to places within six miles of Toronto. All orders sent to T. F. Cary, 68 King Street West, will be punctually attended to.

R. B. RICHARDS.

Toronto. June 1, 1854.

An advertisement of Richard B. Richard's ice business appeared in the Provincial Freeman, *July 8, 1854.*

summer months. Mr. Richards employed his children and other relatives in his business and on the farm.

Reverend Mitchell, a neighbour and acquaintance, described the Richards' business concerns as follows:

An ice merchant, who furnishes hotels, public houses, and private families, during the summer with ice, has a farm under good cultivation. His son-in-law has on the same farm a two-story frame house, furnished as well inside as it is finished outside.

R.B. Richards was a respected member and trustee of the Coloured Regular Baptist Church on Terauley and Edward streets in St. John's Ward, Toronto, the same church where Reverend Mitchell served and that was attended by Adophus Judah and his family.

THE CARY BROTHERS

The Cary brothers, George W., Isaac N., John I. and Thomas, were free-born Blacks from Virginia who came to Toronto in the 1840s. They opened several barber saloons which catered to all Torontonians. In the 1850s, Thomas joined with Richard B. Richards in the ice business. By 1854, Cary and Richards owned four ice houses; Thomas, however, continued to operate the barber shop with his brothers. They advertised in the *Provincial Freeman*:

... all who wish to be operated upon in the line of either hair cutting, shaving, hair curling or shampooing."

The Cary brothers were also strong abolitionists. They campaigned against racial prejudice, led black self-help organizations, organized Black conventions, and urged the city's Blacks to abandon the Conservative Party and support George Brown's Reform Party or the Liberals. In 1857, Thomas married Mary Ann Shadd Cary, publisher of the *Provincial Freeman*, and Isaac N. married Mary Bibb, widow of Henry Bibb. William Wells Brown, an abolitionist writer, described Isaac as "one of the most enterprising and intellectual men in Canada, [who] is deeply interested in the moral, social, and political elevation of all classes."

MARY ANN SHADD

Mary Ann Shadd was perhaps the best-known female abolitionist in Canada. Born in Wilmington, Delaware, of free Black parents, she was the daughter of Abraham Shadd, a respected abolitionist and leader of the Black convention movement. The family moved to Pennsylvania so that Mary Ann and her siblings could attend a private Quaker school for Black children. After graduating, Mary Ann taught school in various cities in the Northeastern United States but, in 1850, moved to Windsor, Canada West, and opened a school for fugitive Blacks there.

In Windsor, Mary Ann worked with Henry and Mary Bibb, but because they had a disagreement about the administration of her school and, later, other issues, she decided to establish and publish her views in her own newspaper. After putting out a premiere issue in Windsor, she began publishing her weekly paper in Toronto the following year. From its office at 5 King Street East, the *Provincial Freeman* spoke out against slavery and offered information for members of the

Mary Ann Shadd Cary, educator, lawyer and first Black woman publisher of a newspaper in North America.
Courtesy of National Archives of Canada C29977.

Provincial Freeman.

DEVOTED TO ANTI-SLAVERY, TEMPERANCE, AND GENERAL LITERATURE.

"Self-Reliance is the True Mark of Independence."

VOLUME I.	TORONTO, CANADA WEST, SATURDAY, NOVEMBER 11, 1854.	NUMBER 34.

The Provincial Freeman (1853 to c. 1860) was based in Toronto from 1854-55 before being moved to Chatham, Canada West. The paper provided news by and for the Black community of Canada West (Ontario).

African-Canadian community about issues ranging from education to agriculture, racial uplift and self-improvement. Mary Ann had also published *A Plea for Emigration or Notes on Canada West* in 1852 encouraging African Americans to move to Canada. After a year in Toronto, Shadd moved her paper to Chatham and continued it there until the early 1860s.

In 1857, Mary Ann married Thomas F. Cary, a Toronto businessman and partner of Richard B. Richards. They had two children, Sarah and Linton. Even with a family, she continued to tour the province and the northern United States speaking out on behalf of the anti-slavery cause, Canadian emigration and other matters dear to her heart. With the outbreak of the Civil War and the death of her husband in 1860, Mary Ann had the distinction of being the only Black woman recruiting officer for the Union Army. She later became the second Black woman to obtain a law degree from Howard University in Washington DC. She devoted the rest of her life to the cause of the Black community and women's equality in Washington.

ANN MARIA JACKSON

Ann Maria Jackson was a fugitive slave who fled from her Delaware slaveholder in the spring of 1858. Jackson made it to St. Catharines and then to Toronto. Jackson's flight was spectacular because she not only "stole away" herself, but also seven of her children. This was a rare feat indeed when one considers that most of those who fled slavery on the Underground Railroad were young men in their prime, young men most likely to be sold away from their families. It was difficult for women to run away secretly, especially with young children. While in St. Catharines, Jackson was aided

Ann Maria Jackson and her seven children escape from Maryland, a remarkable feat of courage and determination. From William Still, *The Underground Rail Road* (1872) 512. Toronto Public Library, Special Collections, Genealogy & Maps Centre.

by abolitionist Hiram Wilson, who sent her on to Toronto. Once there, members of the anti-slavery society helped her establish herself in the city. Jackson worked as a washerwoman and lived in St. John's Ward.

The Jackson story is not just one of triumph. Tragedy is the other thread that holds this narrative together. Just before her flight, her slave owner had sold two of her children. Jackson's husband, a free man, went mad as a result and died in the Poor House. It was this loss of two children and husband that prompted her to gather her family and risk all in a desperate flight to freedom.

DR. ALEXANDER T. AND MRS. M.O. AUGUSTA

Mrs. M.O. Augusta was a busy and pioneering woman. She owned a "fancy dry goods and dressmaking" establishment at Adelaide and York streets, right in the midst of

NEW DRUG STORE.

CENTRAL MEDICAL HALL.

A. T. AUGUSTA

BEGS to announce to his Friends and the
Public generally, that he has OPENED
the Store on Yonge Street, one door south of
Elm Street, with a New and Choice Selection of
DRUGS, MEDICINES,
Patent Medicines, Perfumery,
DYE-STUFFS, &c.,
and trusts, by strict attention to his business, to
merit a share of their patronage.
Physicians' Prescriptions, accurately prepared.
LEECHES APPLIED.
Cupping, Bleeding, and Teeth extracted.
The Proprietor, or a competent Assistant, always
in attendance.
Toronto, March 30, 1855.   6-1y

The apothecary owned and operated by Dr. A.T. Augusta was advertised in the Provincial Freeman, *October 13, 1855.*

downtown Toronto. From Mrs. Augusta the women of Toronto bought the latest in fashion from "Paris and London." Her husband, Dr. Alexander T. Augusta, was a distinguished Toronto doctor and surgeon. But achieving that position was challenging. Born in Virginia to free Black parents, Dr. Augusta had hoped to study medicine at the University of Pennsylvania but was denied admission because of his race. He then took up private study. Migrating to Toronto in the early 1850s, he studied medicine at the University of Toronto and graduated in 1860 with a medical degree from Trinity College. He went into private practice, worked at the Toronto Hospital, and was supervisor of the "House of Industry" or the Poor House. In addition, Dr. Augusta owned and operated a pharmacy on Yonge Street just north of Dundas. An anti-slavery activist, A.T. Augusta helped found The Provincial Association for the Education and Elevation of the Colored People of Canada.

In 1863, Dr. Augusta was to be found on the battlefields of the American Civil War. He became the army's first Black doctor; and also held the rank of Major. After the war, Augusta remained in Washington to help establish the Freedmen's Hospital and the medical school at Howard University where he taught medicine. The Augustas made significant business, social and cultural contributions to the City of Toronto.

THOMAS SMALLWOOD

Thomas Smallwood was born in Maryland in 1801 and obtained his freedom, along with that of his sister, at the age of thirty years. Smallwood migrated to Canada West in 1843. His interesting personality is known because he wrote his autobiography, A *Narrative of Thomas W.F. Smallwood, Colored Man*, in 1851. It detailed his life as an enslaved man, his work as an Underground Railroad conductor, and his experiences in Toronto and Ontario. Smallwood, a leader in the Black and abolitionist communities, owned a saw manufacturing business in Toronto.

Thomas Smallwood was one of the key organizers of the Convention of Coloured People held at Drummondville (now Niagara Falls) in August 1847. He was also a delegate at the 1851 North American Convention of Coloured People in Toronto and served as one of its vice-presidents. Smallwood helped organize the Emancipation Day events in the city, was a shareholder of the *Provincial Freeman*, and was one of the founders of the Provincial Union Association.

A

NARRATIVE

OF

THOMAS SMALLWOOD,

(Coloured Man:)

GIVING AN ACCOUNT

OF HIS

BIRTH—THE PERIOD HE WAS HELD IN SLAVERY—HIS
RELEASE—AND REMOVAL TO CANADA, ETC.

TOGETHER WITH

AN ACCOUNT OF THE UNDERGROUND RAILROAD.

WRITTEN BY HIMSELF.

Toronto:

PRINTED FOR THE AUTHOR BY JAMES STEPHENS, 5, CITY
BUILDINGS, KING STREET EAST.
1851.

Title page of Thomas Smallwood's book. From Thomas Smallwood, A Narrative of Thomas Smallwood *(Coloured Man)* (Toronto: Thomas Smallwood, 1851. Reprinted in Toronto by Mercury Press, 2000,21. Richard Almonte, ed.). Used with permission of Mercury Press.

850-60

Yorkville Bus Line. City of Toronto Archives, TTC Fonds, Series 71, Item 10179.

II How Do We Know?

One of the questions people often ask about history is, "How do you know so much about things that happened such a long time ago?" Finding out about life in 19th century African-Canadian Toronto is difficult because many of the people of the time, both Black and white, could not read or, more importantly, write. So there is no account of their own experiences, recorded in what historians call "their own voice." Also, historians have only recently become interested in the everyday lives of the ordinary people, who worked, and raised families, and died without ever doing anything to get their names in the newspaper.

There are very few books written about early Black life in Ontario, and none yet on Toronto. In fact, this is the very first! Some books about Toronto do mention that Black people, many of them fugitive slaves, used to live there. But that's about it. So we have to delve deeper to discover the African-Canadian story. Fortunately, with the significant number of Black people living in the city by 1860, some records just have to exist.

The first place we look for information is the census, which was the government's attempt to count every single person living in Canada in that year. These were done more or less every ten years. Although the 1851 census for the City of Toronto has been lost, there are some official records, at least for every year starting with 1821. There were also unofficial counts of the urban population, and several of the city's Black population, that we can examine as well. The census is the only document that regularly identifies whether a person was Black or white, the names of everyone living in the household, where they were born and what they did for a living.

Another document that is very helpful is the *Toronto Street and Business Directory*. Starting in 1833, these books were like phone books without the phone numbers. They listed every householder in the city, where they lived and what they did for a living. Sometimes they also had the word "coloured" in brackets after a person's name, although this was not always done consistently.

Once someone's address has been found, more information is contained in the city Tax Assessment rolls. Some Toronto tax rolls also note whether people were of African origin and where they had been born. Chances are that someone listed as "Black" or "mulatto" (of mixed parentage) who had been born in Virginia or Kentucky was once a slave, and it is possible that he or she came to Toronto on the Underground Railroad.

Checking these documents against each other over a number of years can give an idea when people arrived in the city first, and perhaps when they either moved away or died. Checking cemetery records from the Toronto Necropolis and various churches is helpful because these give the exact date of death, the cause, the officiating minister and the name of the person who purchased the burial plot.

From this point, the sources for information can really vary quite widely. Most church baptismal, marriage and death records for Toronto's early African-Canadian churches have been lost, but Black families attending Anglican, Roman Catholic or Presbyterian services would have had important events recorded.

School board records give the name of every child who went to school. These are preserved in the Toronto District School Board Archives, although the ethnic background of the children was not noted. The records of students attending the Toronto Normal School (where teachers were trained), the various colleges of the University of Toronto and private schools such as Upper Canada College are available. So are lists of Black men in the militia and in the army at various periods, including the Union Army in the Civil War.

Of course, important families and those whose descendants are still living in Toronto may have available collections of business and family papers, including letters, family Bibles, diaries and photographs. The Abbott Papers in the Baldwin Room of the Toronto Reference Library are a treasure trove. Historian Daniel Hill gathered copies of a large amount of pictures and documents; the originals remain in private hands. The Daniel Hill Papers are divided between the National Archives of Canada and the Ontario Archives. The latter also holds the very significant personal collection of Alvin McCurdy, an Amherstburg-area historian of African Canada.

Black newspapers such as Henry Bibb's *Voice of the Fugitive* and Mary Ann Shadd's *Provincial Freeman* are invaluable resources for the study of this topic. Other Toronto newspapers such as the *Colonial Advocate*, the *Leader* and the *Patriot* expressed opinions on the larger events of the day, while George Brown's *Globe* was a strong and constant voice supporting the anti-slavery struggle.

Finally, the Ontario Black History Society has for many years gathered together information about the history of African Canadians living in this province. A great deal of the materials in the OBHS collection have been donated by families and individuals whose ancestors were fugitive slaves and free Black immigrants in the 19th century.

Notes

INTRODUCTION

1. Benjamin Drew, *The Refugee: Or The Narratives of Fugitive Slaves in Canada* (Boston, 1856) 94.
2. The Fugitive Slave Law passed by the American government in 1850 expanded the ability of the government to protect the interests of slaveholders. This law required the capture and return to their owners of all fugitive slaves, even those who had escaped the South and made their way to Northern States.

CHAPTER 2: BLACKS IN EARLY TORONTO

1. Edith G. Firth, *The Town of York, 1793-1815: A Collection of Documents of Early Toronto*, Volume 1 (Toronto: University of Toronto Press, 1962) lxxviii.
2. The War of 1812 was a conflict between Britain (including Canada) and the United States (1812 to 1814). Most of the fighting occurred along the Canadian border as the Americans unsuccessfully tried to annex British North America, to make it part of the United States.

CHAPTER 3: UNDERGROUND RAILROAD TO TORONTO

1, This story also appears in W.M. Mitchell's *The Underground Rail Road* (pp. 4-5), which also includes the quotation as used.
2. From 1793 to 1841, the province of Ontario was known as Upper Canada. Between 1841 and 1867, it was called Canada West. In 1867, the year of Canada's Confederation, it became Ontario.

CHAPTER 9: BLACK TORONTONIANS IN THE CIVIL WAR

1. In the last two decades of the nineteenth century (1880s and 1890s) and the early decades of the twentieth, American states began enacting laws that solidified what came to be known as "segregation." Black people were no longer permitted to share railway cars, streetcars and buses, public washrooms, theatres, restaurants, schools and other public facilities with white people. It was only in the 1960s, with the rise of the Civil Rights Movement, that these harsh and restrictive laws were removed. They were called Jim Crow laws because of a famous character from the 1830s – a white actor who blackened his face with shoe polish or lamp blacking and danced and sang pretending to be a happy, silly southern slave. This very insulting stereotype came to be used as the title for all repressive laws and customs that white Americans imposed on Black Americans.

For Further Reading

Alexander, Ken & Avis Glaze, *Towards Freedom: The African-Canadian Experience*. Toronto: Umbrella Press, 1996.

Armstrong, F.H., "The Toronto Directories and the Negro Community In The Late 1840's" *Ontario History*, Volume LXI, 2 (June 1969).

_____, *Toronto: The Place of Meeting*. Toronto: Windsor Publications, 1993.

Bristow, Peggy, Dionne Brand, Linda Carty, Afua Cooper, Sylvia Hamilton, Adrienne Shadd, *"We're Rooted Here and They Can't Pull Us Up": Essays in African Canadian Women's History*. Toronto: University of Toronto Press, 1994.

Drew, Benjamin, *The Refugee: Or The Narrative of Fugitive Slaves in Canada*. Boston: 1854; Reprint 1970, Coles Reprint Series.

Elgersman, Maureen, *Unyielding Spirits: Black Women and Slavery in Early Canada and Jamaica*. New York: Garland Publishing, 1999.

Firth, Edith, *Town of York, A Collection of Documents of Early Toronto*, Vols. 1 & 2. Toronto: University of Toronto Press, 1952.

Hill, Daniel G., "The Blacks in Toronto," in Robert F. Harney, ed., *Gathering Place: Peoples and Neighbourhoods of Toronto, 1834-1945*. Toronto: Multicultural History Society of Ontario, 1985, 75-105.

_____, *The Freedom-Seekers: Blacks in Early Canada*. Agincourt: The Book Society of Canada, 1981.

_____, "Negroes in Toronto, 1793-1865" *Ontario History*, Vol. LV (1963), No. 2.

Hill, Lawrence, *Any Known Blood*. Toronto: HarperCollins, 1997.

_____, *Women of Vision: Canadian Negro Women's Association 1951-1976*. Toronto: Umbrella Press, 1996.

Meyler, Peter ed., *Broken Shackles: Old Man Henson From Slavery to Freedom*. Toronto: Natural Heritage Books, 2001.

Meyler, Peter & David, *A Stolen Life: Searching for Richard Pierpoint*. Toronto: Natural Heritage Books, 1999.

Mitchell, Rev. W.M., *The Under-Ground Railroad*. Westport, Connecticut: Negro Universities Press, 1860, reprinted 1970.

Ripley, C. Peter, *Black Abolitionist Papers, Volume II: Canada, 1830-1865*. Chapel Hill: University of North Carolina Press, 1986.

Robinson, David & Douglas Smith, *Sources of the African Past*. New York: Africana Publishing Company, 1979.

Scadding, Henry D.D., *Toronto of Old: Collections and Recollections*. Toronto: Adam, Stevenson & Co., 1873; F.H. Armstrong, ed., Toronto: Dundurn Press, 1987 reprint.

Siebert, Wilbur, *The Underground Railroad from Slavery to Freedom*. New York: Arno Press, [1898] 1968.

Silverman, Jason, *Unwelcome Guests: The White Canadian Response to American Fugitive Slaves, 1860-1865*. New York: Associated Faculty Press, 1985.

Smallwood, Thomas, *A Narrative of Thomas Smallwood (Coloured Man 1851)*. Reprint Richard Almonte, ed. Toronto: Mercury Press, 2000.

Still, William, *The Underground Rail Road*. Philadelphia: Porter & Coates, 1872; Chicago: Johnson Publishing Company Inc., reprint 1970.

Stouffer, Allen, *The Light of Nature and the Law of God: Antislavery in Ontario 1833-1877*. Baton Rouge: Louisiana State University Press, 1992.

Walker, James W. St. G., *A History of Blacks in Canada: A Study Guide for Teachers and Students*. Hull, Quebec: Minster of State Multiculturalism, 1980.

Ward, Samuel Ringgold, *Autobiography of a Fugitive Negro: His Anti-Slavery Labors in the United States, Canada & England*. Chicago: Johnson Publishing Company, [1855] 1970.

Wayne, Michael, "The Myth of the Fugitive Slave: The Black Population of Canada West on the Eve of the Civil War," L'Histoire Sociale/Social History, Vol. 28, No. 56 (November 1995) 465-481.

Winks, Robin, *The Blacks in Canada: A History*. Montreal: McGill-Queen's University Press and London, U.K. and New Haven, Conn.: Yale University Press, 1971.

Suggestions for Junior Readers

Ayres, Katherine, *North By Night: A Story of the Underground Railroad*. New York: Delacorte Press, 1998.

Carbone, Elisa, *Stealing Freedom*. New York: Knopf, 1998.

Girard, Linda, *Young Frederick Douglass*. Illinois: Morton Grove Press, 1994.

Gorrell, Gena K., *The Story of the Underground Railroad*. Toronto: Stoddart Publishing, 1996. Now available through Fitzhenry & Whiteside.

Granfield, Linda, *Amazing Grace: The Story of the Hymn*. Toronto: Tundra Books, 1997.

Greenwood, Barbara, *The Last Safe House: A Story of the Underground Railroad*. Toronto: Kids Can Press, 1998.

Haskins, James & Kathleen Benson, *Building a New Land: African Americans in Colonial America*. New York: HarperCollins, 2001.

Hill, Lawrence, *Trials and Triumphs: The Story of African-Canadians*. Toronto: Umbrella Press, 1993.

Jenkins, Earnestine, *A Glorious Past: Ancient Egypt, Ethiopia and Nubia*. New York: Chelsea House, 1995.

Krass, Peter, *Sojourner Truth, Anti-Slavery Activist*. Los Angeles: Melrose Square Publishing, 1988.

Kristof, Jane, *Steal Away Home*. New York: Avon Books, 1969.

Lemelle, Sid, *Pan Africanism for Beginners*. New York: Writers & Readers, 1992.

McKissack, Patricia, *Nzingha, Warrior Queen of Matamba*. New York: Scholastic Inc., 2000.

Paulsen, Gary, *Nightjohn*. New York: Delacourt Press, 1993.

Ringgold, Faith, *Aunt Harriet's Underground Railroad in the Sky*. New York: Crown Publishers, 1992.

Sadlier, Rosemary, *Mary Ann Shadd: Publisher-Editor-Teacher-Lawyer-Suffragette*. Toronto: Umbrella Press, 1995.

_____, *Tubman: Harriet Tubman and the Underground Railroad*. Toronto: Umbrella Press, 1997.

Schwartz, Virginia Frances, *If I Just Had Two Wings*. Toronto: Fitzhenry & Whiteside, 2001.

Schroeder, Alan and Jerry Pinckney, *Minty: A Story of Young Harriet Tubman*. New York: Dial Books for Young Readers, 1996.

Smucker, Barbara, *Underground to Canada*. Toronto: Clarke Irwin, 1977.

Winter, Jeanette, *Follow the Drinking Gourd*. New York: Knopf, 1998.

Wisniewski, David, *Sundiata: Lion King of Mali*. New York: Clarion Books, 1992.

Wright, Courtney C., *Jumping the Broom*. New York: Holiday House, 1994.

Selected Poetry for the Young Reader

Brand, Dionne, *Earth Magic*. Toronto: Sister Vision Press, 1993.

Cooper, Afua, *The Red Caterpillar on College Street*. Toronto: Sister Vision Press, 1989.

Rochelle, Brenda, *Words With Wings: A Treasury of African-American Poetry and Art*. New York: HarperCollins, 2001.

Index

About the Authors

From l-r: Karolyn Smardz Frost, Afua Cooper and Adrienne Shadd. Photo by Alpha Diallo.

Adrienne Shadd is a freelance researcher, writer, curator and editor living in Toronto. She is co-author of *"We're Rooted Here and They Can't Pull Us Up": Essays in African Canadian Women's History* (University of Toronto Press, 1994) and co-editor of *Talking About Difference: Encounters in Culture, Language and Identity* and *Talking About Identity: Encounters in Race, Ethnicity and Language* (Between the Lines, 1994 and 2001), with Carl James. Most recently, she curated an exhibition on the experience of African-Canadian workers in the twentieth century.

Afua Cooper's doctoral dissertation on Henry Bibb is a pioneering work on the life of the 19th-century abolitionist. She has taught Caribbean, Canadian and Women's history at the University of Toronto, York University and Ryerson University and is co-author of *"We're Rooted Here and They Can't Pull Us Up": Essays in African Canadian Women's History*. In February 2002, Afua curated "A Glimpse of Black Life in Victorian Toronto: 1850-1860" for the City of Toronto Museum Division. This exhibit ran at Mackenzie House Museum for seven months. It is now showcased at the Rotunda, Toronto's City Hall. An award-winning poet, she has published four books of poetry. Her latest release is a CD of Dub Poetry entitled *Worlds of Fire*.

Karolyn Smardz Frost is a historian and professional archaeologist who specializes in the Underground Railroad. A widely published writer on African-Canadian history, public archaeology and multicultural education, and the former Vice-Chair of the Toronto Historical Board, she is completing her doctorate in the History of Race and Slavery, under the supervision of Dr. James W. St.G. Walker at the University of Waterloo. She directed, until its demise in 1995, the Toronto District School Board's internationally acclaimed Archaeological Resource Centre, the pilot project of which was the excavation of the Thornton and Lucie Blackburn fugitive slave homestead. Her biography of this remarkable couple, *Goin' to Freedom Land*, is being published by Farrar, Straus and Giroux of New York in 2004.

Over a two-year period, Adrienne, Afua and Karolyn worked on the research for the ROM exhibit, "The Underground Railroad: Next Stop, Freedom!" sponsored by Parks Canada and the Ontario Black History Society. This book is based on their research for this project.